BLACK IVY

BLACK IVY

A REVOLT IN STYLE

JASON JULES   GRAHAM MARSH

R|A|P

REEL ART PRESS

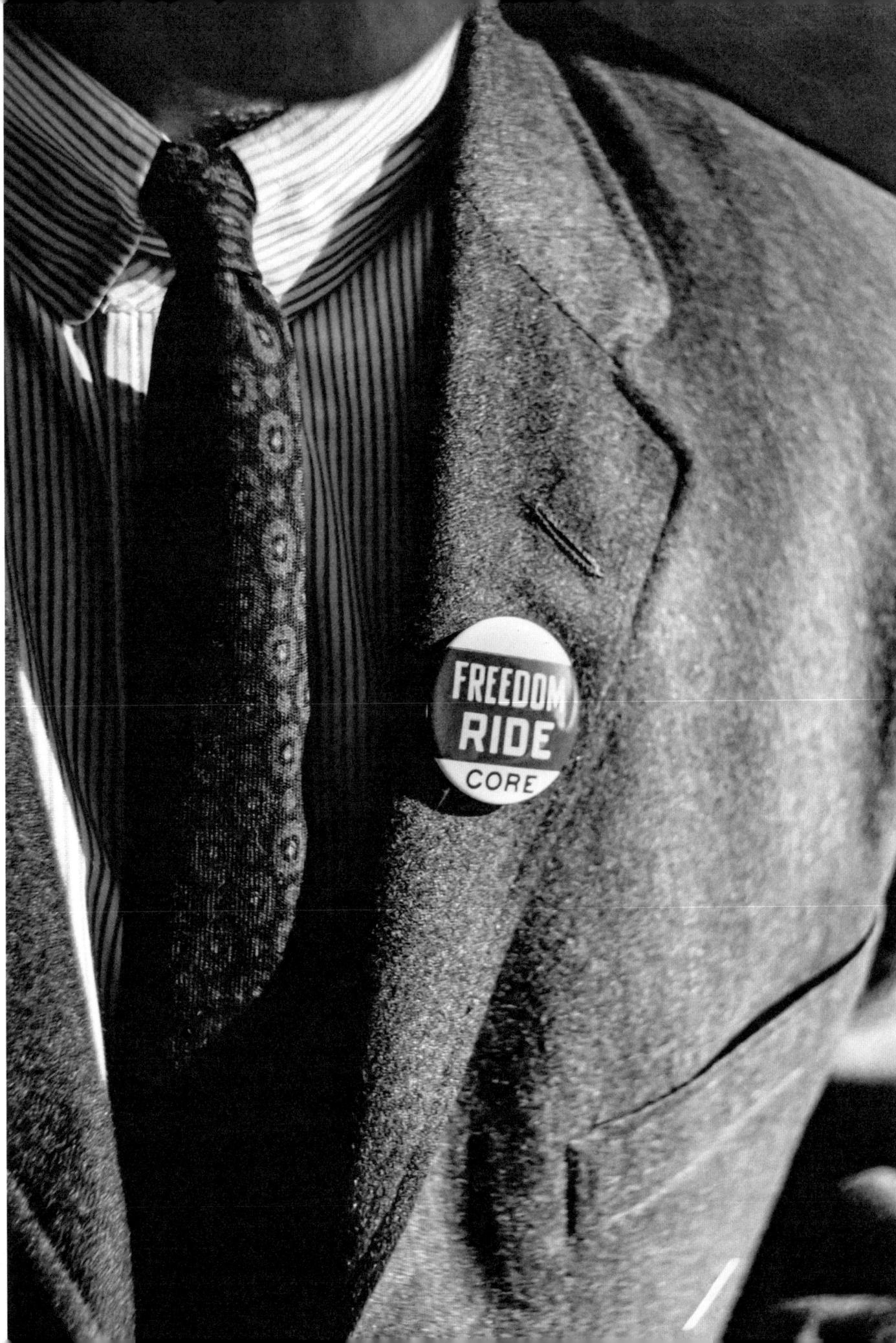

A REVOLT IN STYLE

JASON JULES

Style is about the freedom to be oneself, to authentically express oneself, and in doing so reject limitations imposed by others. A consciousness of style, in essence, emerges when one asserts one's right to self-definition and the right to take control of one's own identity.

This is a story about menswear. This is an untold story about style. A revolt in style.

It's a story about a generation of people challenging the status quo, demanding racial equality and civil rights. It's the story of one of the most volatile and incendiary periods in American history, but it's also a story about dignity and the fight for self-determination. For the first time, we explore the major role this style of clothing played during this period of upheaval and social change, and what these clothes said about the men who wore them.

When it comes to this period and these clothes, it's often mistakenly argued that Black men appropriated this style out of a desire to be white, coming from a deep sense of inferiority. In reality, the urge to wear these clothes was in no small part borne of the desire to demonstrate that equality which had been so fiercely denied them in other ways. Countering racist preconceptions, the goal was to be recognized as at least equal to the rights they were fighting for, not only in the eyes of the American mainstream but throughout the world. Rather than a sign of conformity and compliance, Black Ivy was a kind of battledress, a symbolic armour worn in the nonviolent pursuit of fundamental change. Making society treat them differently meant making the mainstream see them differently first. And they did.

Dressing in Ivy style was not new to Black society. In places like Washington, Chicago, New Jersey, and Harlem during the years between the First and Second World Wars, many Black professionals wore the Ivy look of the day. In fact, for years, Black leader W.E.B. Du Bois, who also studied at Harvard, had an account at Brooks Brothers, and he'd regularly have tailor-made suits and shirts from their Madison Avenue store delivered to his home. And a young Miles Davis, his father being a doctor, was more than familiar with the style

Synonymous with the civil rights movement, this raised seam, wool jacket, tab collar shirt, medallion pattern tie, and pin badge combination is also a neat shorthand for Black Ivy. **JJ**

from a very early age. But the Black Ivy style of the late 1950s and '60s was more than just about clothes or fashion. It was a kind of sartorial power grab, that in many ways had as much visual impact as the Black Panthers' beret, rifle, and leather jacket that shot up in its wake.

Originally the goal was to convey an attitude of equity and structure within the creative context of musicians and artists, to present themselves as worthy of being taken seriously as artists. Then with the emergence of the civil rights movement, the look took another turn; still premised on the idea of equality and respect, it became synonymous with activism and progressive thinking. In this way, the Ivy look was integrated into the language of rebellion and subversion, challenging the status quo while at the same time honouring it. To honour the status quo? That, after all, was the intention, to have equal rights within the already established democratic and economic system, not to overturn it. At least not initially, anyway.

To many in mainstream America, particularly supporters of Jim Crow and those who believed that African Americans were inferior to whites, this image presented them with an overwhelming cognitive dissonance, upending the firmly held belief that Black people were to present themselves as underlings.

Within the look itself, there's a wealth of variations that spin out of the initial Ivy foundation. Many of these variations come from the unique experiences of the Black Ivyists themselves, while others are simply responses to the needs and conditions of the times. As a result, Black Ivy style became a thing in and of itself, distinct from Ivy but always related to it. Ironically, the characterisation of Ivy league clothing as quintessentially cool is due in no small part to the enormous, but until now undocumented, influence Black Ivy style has had on mainstream culture—past and present.

The old adage, it's not what you wear it's how you wear it, is never truer than in the case of Black Ivy style, where the classic Ivy wardrobe was comprehensively raided and then remixed and re-envisioned, away from its elitist confines, away from its mass-market popularity, and into something heavily coded and intentionally revolutionary.

Keeping things cool. It's almost impossible to understand the continued relevance of the Ivy style without taking into account the influence Black culture had on the look in the late 1950s and '60s. JJ

THE BIRTH OF COOL

GRAHAM MARSH

'Dressing Fine, Making Time'. This line from Dobie Gray's song, 'The "In" Crowd', just about summed up the British modernist ethic in the early 1960s for me. Haircuts from France, scooters from Italy, clothes from the United States, all nailed down with a laconic London attitude. The importance of being imported applied to the clothes as much as to the music. While modern jazz and the soul that poured out of the Stax, Atlantic, and Motown record labels, plus a side order of Ska and Blue Beat, was required listening, the desired look for discerning modernists was strictly Ivy League.

For a white South London mod, at the time working in London's Fleet Street at a publishing company called Hulton Press with a bunch of like-minded Ivy pilgrims, our musical and sartorial heroes were Black Americans. However, there was one outfit at the time that made a lasting impression and that was The Modern Jazz Quartet, simply known as the MJQ. A French movie called *Sait-on Jamais...* (a literal translation of which is *One Never Knows*) was released in the States as *No Sun in Venice* (1957). It was directed by Roger Vadim and had an original score by John Lewis, the pianist leader of the MJQ. The other members of the quartet were Milt Jackson, vibraharp; Percy Heath, bass; and Connie Kay, drums. Apart from being superb musicians, their clothes were sharper than a Gillette razor blade. There was one very cool track on the *No Sun in Venice* album, entitled 'The Golden Striker', that was inspired by a familiar tourist site in Venice—the life-sized figures on one of the buildings near St. Mark's Cathedral that revolve around and strike the hours—and it became a kind of modernist anthem. It's worth owning the album for the cover alone, which used a J.M.W. Turner painting of the view of the Grand Canal in Venice.

Whether riffing on the threads that Miles Davis wore—he was, after all, the modernist's ideal, the essence of Ivy hipness—or listening to the groundbreaking chords that the

John Coltrane arriving at Schiphol Airport in 1960. He was in Amsterdam for a series of concerts with Miles Davis. Looking every inch the seasoned traveller in a soft Ivy jacket, candy-stripe button-down and a woollen cardigan. **GM**

genius of modern music, Thelonious Monk, played, a lot of time was spent 'topping up', which meant always being able to be one up on others. OK, it might be seen now as a shallow pursuit, but back then tracking down rare Blue Note albums and wearing the correct button-down and tab-collared shirts was essential to one's Ivy credibility. That, and spending lunch times at the Lyceum, which was just off the Strand in London's West End, listening to Ray Charles and proto-cool collections of rare groove records being played.

The modernist clubs that were based in London's Soho attracted many Black American GIs who were stationed in the UK in the '60s, and integrated audiences were the norm. As long as you looked sharp and dug the music, anything else was just jiving, there was strictly no room for squares. An additional bonus for the mods was a constant supply of genuine Levi's 501s and Made in USA button-down shirts, all courtesy of the GIs and their PX stores.

In 1991 I co-authored and art-directed a book called *The Cover Art of Blue Note Records*. With their unfailing taste, Blue Note covers managed to distil all the artistic influences the United States had to offer during the middle decades of the twentieth century. Founded by label bosses Alfred Lion and Francis Wolff, Blue Note was an impressive catalogue of outstandingly hip African-American musical talent. The covers elegantly encapsulated all that had been happening in post-war graphic design on an increasingly accessible 12-and-a-half-inch square of cardboard. Blue Note covers also served another purpose, providing a peerless, photographic guide to the Ivy look clothes the musicians wore—which, in the '60s in South London, was very important.

Having been obsessed with Ivy clothing and accessories for more years than I care to remember, I agreed completely when Jason suggested we do a book on Black Ivy. Tony Nourmand, who I have co-authored and art-directed many books with, is the editor-in-chief of Reel Art Press and agreed to green light the project. *Black Ivy* digs deep into the archives to produce the ultimate guide to the genuine article, it's a subject that has been somewhat neglected—that is until now...

The Last King of America— How Miles Davis Invented Modernity: that was writer Gerald Early's title for a 3,000 word piece that he wrote on Miles Davis. In this moody photograph by Jean-Pierre Leloir, Davis wears a beautiful foulard patterned button-down with a plain tie under an immaculately tailored suit. His attitude was a big influence on the Ivy community. **GM**

IN LITERATURE

THE VANGUARD OF WORD AND SOUND

The style of **TED JOANS** (1928–2003), like his poetry, links Beat culture to an emerging Black consciousness. His beret, a classic signature of the Beats, along with the dishevelled style of his clothes in both images, is unquestionably Beat, while the clothes themselves are pure Ivy. What's interesting to remember is that while the Beatniks, with figureheads such as Jack Kerouac, Allen Ginsberg, and William Burroughs (with whom Joans was friends) are seen as creating and defining the Beatnik movement, many of their cultural reference points and inspirations were Black, including musical heroes such as Charlie Parker and Billie Holiday. Joans was himself a former roommate of Charlie Parker's and is renowned for having coined the term 'Bird Lives!', upon hearing of the bebop legend's death. Here, Joans is pictured in 1957 outside New York's Cafe Bizarre, and also performing inside the venue. **JJ**

LeRoi Jones

AMIRI BARAKA/IMAMU AMEAR BARAKA (1934–2014)

The playwrite, poet, renowned jazz aficionado, intellectual and political activist was ever moving forward. But with all those changes, his style often had a classic air to it, it might even be ascribed to librarian or college professor, such was its iconic bookishness. Although it seemed to take its lead from the most trad of Ivy look wardrobes, you'll notice that on closer inspection something else is actually at work here. While each item of clothing looks conventional enough, orthodox even, there's a kind of dishevelled aspect to it, a kind of ill-fittedness that really speaks less of trad and more of Beat. Baraka, or as he was called at that time LeRoi Jones, explores the Ivy style through the prism of the Beat poet and Beatnik culture. JJ

Opposite: A modernist in the true sense, Baraka is pictured here in a photograph by Burt Glinn, sitting outside his Brownstone in Newark, New Jersey, in 1959, wearing a blue button-down chambray shirt, pair of chinos, and suede boots. Notice how beautifully beat the chinos are. *Above:* An image taken in 1963, Baraka wears a plaid button-down with a knitted shawl collar cardigan. As in the previous image, a white t-shirt is worn underneath the shirt and is just peeking through. Despite the informality of his clothes, he is immaculately groomed, as if to say, he may be Beat, but he certainly isn't beaten. JJ

THE BAPTISM & THE TOILET
BY LEROI JONES

EVERGREEN PLAYSCRIPT

Opposite: Here in 1964 is Baraka wearing shades and a woven jacket, fully buttoned, with a dark shirt and tie. It's the opening night of one of his now infamous plays, *The Toilet*. *Left:* The modernist cover for both *The Toilet* and *The Baptism*, both plays explore questions of manhood, sexuality, race, and acceptance. **JJ**

Like many Black Ivyists, **RALPH ELLISON (1913–1994)** had a seemingly conservative dress code, which might appear to run at odds with his modernist, consciousness-shifting creative output. At least, that is, until you realise that resolving this existential dichotomy is at the very heart of his work. *Invisible Man* is about a search for identity and the fundamental need for self-definition. Published in 1952, it quickly became essential reading among civil rights activists, and then later for members of the Black Power movement. *Right:* It's hard to imagine the guy in this photograph from 1966, dressed in a patch pocket sports coat, a military repp tie, and a felt trilby could have so much radical swing, but there it is. *Opposite:* The trench coat will forever be part of African-American style, immortalized by both Richard Roundtree as Shaft, and also Marvin Gaye on the cover of the *What's Going On* album. Originally introduced by British brand Burberry in the early 1900s, it came into its own during the First World War when it was adopted by the British military. The functionality of the trench coat, with the inherent masculinity of the design, had obvious appeal to purveyors of Black Ivy style. The trench conveyed a sense of strength and sophistication, two important factors in the Black Ivy aesthetic. Here, Ellison sports a classic British military trench coat to full effect. **JJ**

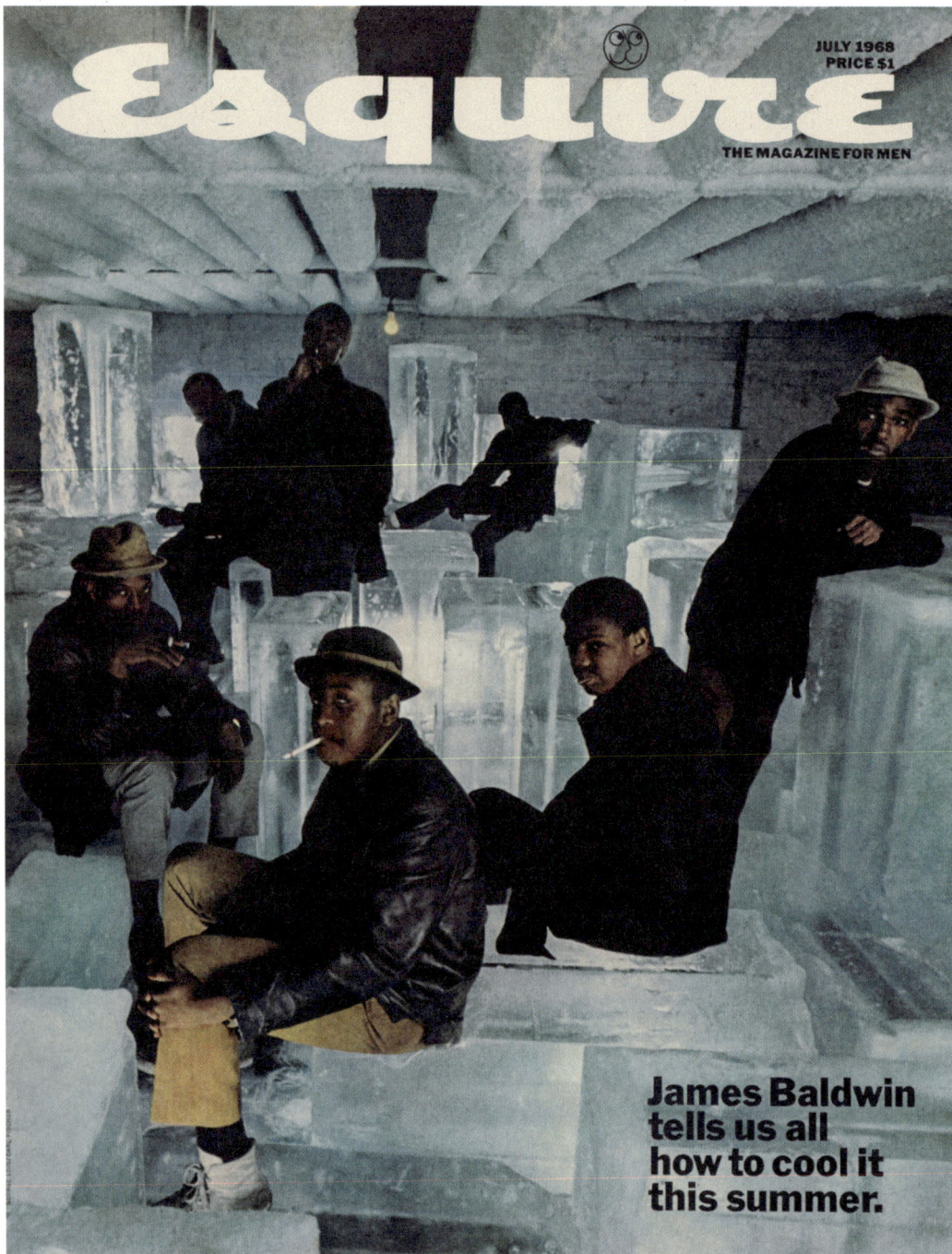

Esquire

JULY 1968
PRICE $1

THE MAGAZINE FOR MEN

James Baldwin
tells us all
how to cool it
this summer.

Opposite: The epitome of defiance and style, there's writer and activist **JAMES BALDWIN (1924–1987)** pictured in Durham, North Carolina. Baldwin, known for his style even then, is wearing an opulent shearling coat, capable of resisting the worst of New York winters, a dark suit, a white shirt with slim tie, and a pair of nubuck monk strap winter boots. Incredibly popular at the time, variations of the shearling were also notably worn by Marlon Brando in *On The Waterfront,* James Dean in *Giant* and Steve McQueen in *The War Lover. Left:* Baldwin's cover story, published just after the killing of Martin Luther King, Jr. It features young Black men in an industrial size icebox, while the story within discusses how Black people can refrain from rioting or *cool it*, to use the common term of the time, in a response to the assassination of King. 'How can we get the Black people to cool it?' *Esquire* asks. 'It is not for us to cool it', Baldwin replies. 'But aren't you the ones who are getting hurt the most?', says *Esquire*. 'No', Baldwin says, 'we are only the ones who are dying fastest'. JJ

Opposite: There's **ALEX HALEY (1921–1992)**, co-author of Malcolm X's autobiography, writer of the groundbreaking and somewhat controversial book *Roots*, and possibly the only *Playboy* journalist ever to be interviewed by the magazine. This might come as no surprise since Haley was *Playboy*'s first ever interviewer. His debut piece? An incendiary Q&A with Miles Davis in 1962. He would later file interviews for the magazine with Quincy Jones, Martin Luther King, Muhammad Ali (then Cassius Clay), and American Nazi Party leader George Lincoln Rockwell, among others. Here he is around that period, in a crisp corduroy sports coat, skinny tie and button-down shirt. The elegant curve of his jacket lapel over its top button is a thing of sheer beauty. *Right:* In the world of Black Ivy, wearing glasses was a plus. It says bookishness, intelligence, learning. As a look, it was consistent with the civil rights' non-violent approach, as well as the timeless personal style of Malcolm X. In this respect, spectacles and sunglasses were worn not just out of necessity but also as a powerful style statement, as both Alex Haley and **NATHAN WRIGHT, JR.**, **(1923–2005)**, author of the book *Black Power and Urban Unrest* published in 1968, show here. **JJ**

IN THE ARTS

BECOMING YOUR OWN WITNESS

One of the most important modernist sculptors of the twentieth century, **NOAH PURIFOY (1917–2004)** created his work from found objects, taking Duchamp's seminal credo of the Readymade and developing epic pieces of stature and beauty. He would spend the latter part of his life in the desert, building *The White House*, a veritable Taj Mahal built out of assembled trash in California's iconic Joshua Tree. *Opposite:* Pictured here in the mid '60s, Purifoy deftly manages to echo the porcelain purity of the sink beside him wearing white chinos, shirt, and suede crepe sole shoes. Re-evaluating, elevating, reclaiming that which others reject or ignore is at the core of his practice. In a way, it's meta commentary on the anti-consumerist, side glance satire that fuelled much of the Pop Art of the time. *Right:* The assemblage here illustrates this—a work created from objects found in the wake of the Watts Riots, which took place in the summer of 1965. Again his clothes, a striped short-sleeved button-down shirt, and canvas coloured slacks with brown slip on shoes, somehow manage to echo the sculpture beside him. It was part of a group exhibition that eventually toured the whole of the US, called 66 *Signs of Neon.* **JJ**

AUGUST 1968 • ISSUED MONTHLY

A SUPPLEMENT TO
CHICAGO SUNDAY SUN-TIMES
Prepared and paid for by Tuesday Publications, Inc.

Tuesday MAGAZINE

A NEW BREED OF CARS: SPECIAL & SPORTY

SUMMER FISHING FOR THE FUN OF IT

THE NEGRO IN WORLD HISTORY GEORGE A. P. BRIDGETOWER

IN WATTS: EDUCATION THROUGH ART / PAGE 4

CHARLES WHITE
(1918–1979) was something close to the Kehinde Wiley of his day. He hung out with the likes of Harry Belafonte, Gordon Parks, Richard Wright, Jacob Lawrence, Langston Hughes, Sammy Davis, Jr., Ossie Davis, Mahalia Jackson, and Sidney Poitier. In 1966 he was the first artist ever commissioned to do a cover for *Ebony* magazine. His work was exhibited across the US and he taught at the prestigious Otis Art Institute in Los Angeles: here his students included Kerry James Marshall, David Hammons, and Richard Wyatt. Needless to say, his book, *Images of Dignity*, was a must read for anyone looking for a serious take on modern art from a Black perspective. *Left:* Wearing a tweed raised seam sports coat, a club collar shirt with a collar pin, and a foulard pattern tie. **JJ**

Opposite: In his studio in 1965, White wears timeless Ivy clothes: his short-sleeve, button-down popover shirt, off-white Levi's, white socks and sneakers is still relevant and wearable to today's Ivy style fraternity. **GM**

There's **JACOB LAWRENCE (1917–2000)** demonstrating two sides of the Ivy look, combining a battered sweatshirt with a madras shirt on the left and reclining in an immaculate herringbone tweed suit on the right. A true modernist, at the age of 24 he became the first African-American artist to be represented by a major New York gallery. Lawrence, a friend and contemporary of Charles White, was inspired by life in his neighbourhood Harlem and described his work as dynamic cubism. **JJ**

Gordon Parks

(1912–2006)

In 1969, Parks was the first African American to direct a major Hollywood movie with his autobiographical film, *The Learning Tree*. Two years later, he directed the seminal feature film *Shaft*, starring Richard Roundtree, igniting a slew of other Black orientated movies in what would quickly become known as the Blaxploitation genre. He would also co-found the Black fashion and lifestyle publication *Essence* magazine.

In the early '60s, however, Parks' work still centred around still photography—both fashion and documentary—including groundbreaking portrait studies of Malcolm X and Muhammad Ali, among others, and shooting for the likes of *Vogue* and *Life* magazine. His first gig for *Life* in 1948 was a study called *Harlem Gang Leader*. Not unlike the kids in Shirley Clarke's film *The Cool World*, this was an eight page photo essay on gang culture among teenagers. The magazine wanted to feature a cover image of the gang leader holding a pistol just fired, with smoke coming from its barrel. *Life* wanted that type of story throughout. Parks refused, insisting on presenting a more developed vision of the gang's members. Representing a rounded version of all his subjects was key to Parks, seeing their condition, the situations that they were compelled to confront in everyday life, rather than defining them by race. Parks didn't allow his sense of dress to be defined by others' racial precepts either, ever. JJ

Above: Gordon Parks looking dapper as Dan sporting a cravat under his soft button-down shirt and jacket. GM

Opposite: Photographed here in the mid '60s with Italian model Benedetta Barzini, Parks style looks as relevant today as it did then. JJ

Opposite: This isn't a book about photography, but without the work of great photographers such as **DON HOGAN CHARLES (1938–2017)** this book could not exist. Hogan Charles, featured here wearing aviator style glasses, a woollen tie, Oxford button-down shirt, and tweed sports coat, is perhaps best known for his iconic image of Malcolm X, automatic rifle in hand, looking through the window of his home in Queens, New York, as well as his documentation of the civil rights movement. In 1964 he became the first ever Black photographer to work for the *New York Times*.

Right: **TED WILLIAMS (1925–2009)**, dressed in classic military style trench coat, was, like Don Hogan Charles, a legendary photographer. He not only shot for *Ebony*, *Playboy*, and *Life*, and took images of the some of the world's greatest musicians, including Billie Holiday and Dizzy Gillespie, he also extensively covered the civil rights movement. **JJ**

IN MUSIC

A NEW DAWN FOR THE BOHEMIAN KNIGHTS

'*For me, music and life are all about style.*'

Outside the legendary
jazz club Cafe Bohemia
in Greenwich Village in
1956. Miles' Quintet did a
residency there, which was
also recorded for Columbia
Records. Note the relaxed
loose fit of the jacket, part of
a continuing riff on basics of
Ivy style that he'd begun to
develop. This looser drape of
the jacket would soon give
way to a more trim, almost
Italian style, fit as Davis, in
true Black Ivy style, took the
language and codes of classic
Ivy and made them his own. JJ

Miles Davis

(1926–1991)

A jazz pioneer, possibly one of the most influential musicians of the twentieth century, Miles Davis was also one of the most influential men in terms of style. As with his music, rather than appropriate different modes of dress, he adopted and adapted them. Constantly evolving, he was not only forever ahead of the curve, he created it. From his seminal collection *Birth of the Cool* to *Kind of Blue*, *Sketches of Spain*, *Porgy and Bess*, and later *On the Corner*, *Bitches Brew*, and *Tutu*, he managed to instill his own restrained but powerful aesthetic value into every new style he engaged with— cool jazz, modal jazz, hard bop, funk, jazz fusion....As his music evolved, so too did his style of dress. **JJ**

The irony is that while many Black Ivyists adopted the style in order to be perceived as acceptable in the eyes of the mainstream, they instead managed to heighten the perceived differences by giving the style an edge and attitude that it would have otherwise lacked. Its continued role as central to the modern man's wardrobe is due in no small part to this element of cool they instilled in the look all those years ago. A prime example of this is Miles Davis, here wearing a blazer, contrast button, raised seamed, soft shoulder, with a military style embroidered patch on the breast pocket, and a pair of light coloured chinos. What might look like standard country club attire on someone else, looks like an unequivocal statement of intent on Davis. This was the late '50s and he was adding the soundtrack to the film *Lift to the Scaffold/Ascenseur pour l'échafaud* (1958) by responding to each scene projected in front of him. This had never been done before. More, it was the first ever major film scored by an African American. JJ

'But you've got to have style in whatever you do—writing, music, painting, fashion, boxing, anything.'

Miles Davis

Opposite: Miles Davis looking pensive in the 30th Street Studio, NYC, during the recording of the album *Kind of Blue*, photographed by Don Hunstein. Davis is wearing a long sleeve popover button-down with a cravat and cross-pocket slim pants. *Right:* Davis wears another classic Ivy popover, this one in a soft jersey fabric. **GM**

The man in the green shirt. Miles Davis was the embodiment of hip and the coolest man on the planet during his Ivy suited period. Davis was christened 'The Warlord of the Weejuns' by the great *Esquire* magazine style commentator George Frazier. GM

RIVERSIDE | RLP 12-242

CONTEMPORARY SERIES

monk's music

thelonious monk septet

with coleman hawkins, art blakey, gigi gryce

PAUL WELLER-PAUL BACON

SPECTROSONIC
HIGH-FIDELITY
ENGINEERING

Thelonious Monk

(1917–1982)

Summer, 1957: Monk, maverick pianist, purveyor of the discordant harmony, and infamous hat wearer, is booked for a week's residency at the Five Spot in New York alongside a young John Coltrane. That one week stint turns into two months of consciousness-shifting performances. For the first time ever in front of an audience, Coltrane explores a technique that would later be called sheets of sound; a convulsive, circular cacophony that transcends any previously known definition of music. An exceptionally hyper-animated Monk kicks back his chair and walks away from his piano dancing and chanting *Col-trane!*, urging the saxophonist and his long, fierce solos ever further into the unknown. Outraged critics call it anti jazz, recognizing that Monk has staged a coup—having been dismantling the status quo for years, he has now invited Coltrane to finish it off. The power dynamic between the artist and the audience has been well and truly flipped. **JJ**

If Miles Davis had the green shirt and Jimmy Smith the excellent sweaters, then Thelonious Monk had the glasses and hats. Most nights at the Five Spot, Village Vanguard, or any of Manhattan's countless jazz clubs, Monk could be seen wearing a formidable array of hats. Taking care of business in a straw conical, chequered cap, or snap brim, this genius of modern music appeared to have a hat for every tune. If you want to know the meaning of cool, check out Monk's appearance in director Bert Stern's 1959 movie, *Jazz on a Summer's Day*. For sure Thelonious Monk was a bona fide original. *Left:* For the cover of his 1957 Riverside album, *Monk's Music*, Thelonious rides his kiddie car wearing a chequered madras cap and a deeply hip pair of sunglasses. The cover photograph is by Paul Weller, designed by Paul Bacon. *Opposite: Mister Chapeau*, the genius of modern music, wearing a fur hat as only he can. **GM**

Alongside Charlie Parker and Bud Powell, **JOHN BIRKS 'DIZZY' GILLESPIE (1917–1993)** was one of the musicians who co-authored bebop. In his later years he adopted the Bahá'í Faith and came to recognize playing an instrument as a form of spiritual worship. He also saw jazz as an essentially African, diasporic expression, one that lacked a signature rhythm because North American slaves were forced to create and communicate musically without any access to the drum. Its ability to adapt to the times is what kept its message relevant to new generations of listeners. He saw himself as part of a lineage of trumpet players—Bunk Johnson, King Oliver, Louis Armstrong, Roy Eldridge, and then himself, followed by Miles Davis and Clifford Brown, Freddie Hubbard, and so on. **JJ**

Dizzy's style of dress, including his more conservative later years, influenced generations of fans. *Left:* Wearing a traditional candy-striped Ivy button-down shirt and skinny tie. *Opposite:* A jazzy batik patterned sports jacket, completing the look with a crazy pipe. **GM**

PRESTIGE
HI-FI   LP 7071

BILLY TAYLOR

section cross section cross section cross section cross section cross section cross sect

There's **BILLY TAYLOR (1921–2010)**, Dr Billy Taylor, all geek god like and cool, looking every bit the jazz intellectual that he was. A pianist, composer, broadcaster, and scholar, his understated style of dress, like his reverence for what he called America's Classical Music, stayed with him throughout his life. Among jazz fans, perhaps Taylor's most acclaimed piece is the song 'I Wish I Knew (How It Would Feel to Be Free)'. First released in 1963, it was quickly adopted as something of an anthem by the civil rights movement. While there are several vocal versions—the most popular being Nina Simone's— Taylor's live instrumental recording, all seven minutes plus of it, is the epitome of the gospel infused, soul jazz genre and testimony to his ability both as a composer and as a performer. **JJ**

The two sides of Billy Taylor: *Left:* A relaxed Mr T in a classic set of Ivy threads. *Opposite:* The formal side of Billy Taylor at his piano, wearing a beautiful blue/ grey suit. **GM**

58

The Modern Jazz Quartet

(1952–1997)

Originally they were called the Milt Jackson Quartet. But then, with the desire to be taken more seriously and play in the often quieter surrounds of a classical concert hall rather than a smoky, boozy, rambunctious nightclub, they elected to go by the rather more catchy moniker of The Modern Jazz Quartet. With that, their style changed too, adopting a sophisticated, cut back Ivy look to go with their sophisticated, cut back sound. The members of the MJQ were (above, left to right) **PERCY HEATH (1923–2005)**, **MILT JACKSON (1923–1999)**, **JOHN LEWIS (1920–2001)**, and **CONNIE KAY (1927–1994)**. JJ

Legendary jazz writer Nat Hentoff recalls in his book, *The Jazz Life,* how after one particular rehearsal the four members of the MJQ spent 15 minutes arguing about what suits to wear for their forthcoming appearance in Philadelphia. In fact, not only did they argue about which suits to wear, but which shoes and accessories would be appropriate for the suits. Hentoff's story goes that one of the group's entourage was overheard saying, 'Are they going to be in *Vogue* magazine again?' JJ

THE M.J.Q.

SOUVENIR BROCHURE   TWO SHILLINGS & SIXPENCE

Hottest 10-piece combo in the neighborhood

Ten instruments? Right. The lad sitting down plays 8 of them. On his Hammond Organ. And believe you us, this group is in demand.

When you hear a band like this one swing out, you certainly see (and hear!) some little-known sides of your young people. In the youngster who plays the Hammond Organ, especially, you find remarkable ability to soak up music quickly. And an unexpected eagerness to work, study and practice.

The Hammond Organ is so easy to learn, a beginner can make rich music in weeks. Many unmatched Hammond inventions—Harmonic Drawbars, Patented Reverberation, Touch-Response Percussion—

help produce the sounds of many instruments; and put the band in business.

Prove it to yourself. Take advantage of our Guaranteed PlayTime Plan (available at most Hammond Organ dealers). You can have a Hammond Organ in your home for 30 days, and 6 lessons, all for just $25. If after 30 days you are not playing the organ to your satisfaction, your $25 will be refunded. Or, when you buy the organ, the $25 is your down payment.

Mail the coupon for free catalog showing all models of Hammond Organs, and information on the Guaranteed PlayTime Plan.

Right: The Modern Jazz Quartet's Percy Heath creates an intellectual mood wearing a bell sleeve alpaca cardigan over a shirt and tie. *Opposite:* An early '60s ad for the mighty Hammond organ, where the clothes manage to sell themselves. **JJ**

JOHNNY COLES   JOE HENDERSON   JOHN PATTON   BEN DIXON

STEREO
THE FINEST IN JAZZ SINCE 1939
84139 BLUE NOTE

'Am I Blue'
GRANT
GREEN

Opposite: **BOBBY HUTCHERSON (1941–2016)** pushes the cardigan envelop out with a crew neck number, with the Alpine style brushed wool and metallic buttons popular at the time.
Above: **GRANT GREEN (1935–1979)** adds his own twist with a shawl collar knit. **JJ**

ERIC DOLPHY (1928–1964) called the musicians of his generation freedom players, drawing a through line between the emerging self awareness and call for equality among African Americans and the music he was pursuing—unscripted, reaching both high and low notes, improvised solos seeking new sounds through intuitive responses. *DownBeat*'s editor, John Tynan, was perhaps the first critic to take issue with this new music, with which Dolphy and Coltrane had become synonymous. In a 1961 article he said, 'I heard a good rhythm section...go to waste behind the nihilistic exercises of the two horns....Coltrane and Dolphy seem intent on deliberately destroying [swing]....They seem bent on pursuing an anarchistic course in their music that can but be termed anti-jazz.' In essence, he heard something that he couldn't recognise coming from a place he felt he had influence over. Indeed, while he may have coined the term 'anti jazz', what he probably meant was that it sounded anti establishment, anti mainstream, and even anti him. **JJ**

Opposite: Dolphy's threads were second to none. He never looked better than wearing this timeless shawl collar cardigan—a good alternative to a jacket—plus the woollen watch cap: they are Ivy knitwear classics. *Right:* Taking five in a batik, short sleeve button-down shirt surrounded by his array of instruments. **GM**

THIS IS OUR MUSIC

THE ORNETTE COLEMAN QUARTET

WITH DONALD CHERRY / ED BLACKWELL / CHARLIE HADEN

STEREO

ATLANTIC 1353   FULL *dynamics-frequency* SPECTRUM

What **ORNETTE COLEMAN (1930–2015)** and his cohorts on stage lacked was any form of insecurity. That's what made them so breathtakingly exciting and also threatening at the same time. It was Coleman who, in 1961, injected the term 'free jazz' into the culture. The title of his sixth album, the term not only described Coleman's process and sound, it also directly spoke to what the very experience of freedom was like. Songs such as Billy Taylor's 'I Wish I Knew (How It Would Feel To Be Free)', albums like Sonny Rollins' *Freedom Suite*, Max Roach's *We Insist! Freedom Now Suite*, and so on, addressed, and in many ways affirmed, the relentless struggle Black people faced. But Coleman's music seemed to expose the listener to a post-struggle mindset. It was bold and confident and had intellectual clarity, and required nothing other than itself for validation. Isn't that what true freedom should feel like? JJ

Left: Legions of Ivy pilgrims bought this album just for the cover, simply because the quartet look so sharp. This excellent 1960 Atlantic album was photographed by Lee Friedlander and designed by PushPin Studio alumni, Loring Eutemey. *Opposite:* Coleman poses for a portrait holding his beloved yellow plastic Selmer alto saxophone. He's wearing a classic crew neck with contrast colour around the neckline, known as tipping. **GM**

John Coltrane

(1926–1967)

They called his music revolutionary, although he never claimed to be one. Like every true modernist, Coltrane believed in the redemptive power of his art, its ability to ignite real, tangible change. Had he lived, he most likely would have gone deeper into his exploration of Eastern religions, philosophies, and music.

These two images, side by side, reflect the kind of duality found in Coltrane's work—the transcendental sense of peace, and the intense, incredibly visceral experience that comes through his music. That blue madras shirt, once a pristine example of Ivy simplicity, is now sweat drenched and dishevelled, more vital than ever. That profile, photographed by William Claxton in front of a classic Motherwell at the Guggenheim Museum, is both intense and calm, structurally solid yet free flowing and full of motion. Like one of his most popular pieces, 'My Favorite Things', Black Ivy style was about taking the accepted vernacular of the period and subverting it, elevating it by way of making it indelibly personal and unique. **JJ**

Above: Coltrane looks every inch a template for the Ivy look wearing a soft shouldered jacket, button-down shirt, and knitted tie. **GM**

Opposite: Introduced into the US in the early '50s by shirtmakers Hathaway, the natural softening of the colour in the madras print that takes place over time with these shirts, much like denim, was as much a selling point for the mainstream as it was for the Black Ivyists. As a textile it was tenacious, weathering the winds of change and surviving intact, nonetheless. **JJ**

QUINCY JONES (B.1933) produced classic albums for everyone from Ray Charles to Michael Jackson, and scored over 30 movies, including *In The Heat of the Night*, *The Getaway*, and *The Color Purple*. The transition from performer in big show style orchestras to artist began during the bebop era. Quincy explained this shifting attitude to presenter Terry Gross in 2001, 'We've heard Stravinsky now, we've done this, and we want to be pure artists. We don't want to entertain anymore, we don't want to sing, we don't want to have to dance and move or entertain an audience.' That attitude soon evolved with a new look and new sounds but the same desire to do more than merely provide a distraction for a paying audience. The new sounds: various branches of bop; hard bop, cool jazz, soul jazz, free jazz. And the new look: Black Ivy. **JJ**

There are really two tried and tested elements that have become the epitome of the Ivy look, and that is shirts and shoes. *Left:* The genuine Ivy-clad composer wearing a very cool pin-collared shirt, these days this collar style is as rare as hens' teeth. *Opposite:* Q has on a pair of plain front Florsheim Imperial cordovan loafers—this model was called Yuma. They had a hand-sewn front, genuine moccasin construction, with leather sole and heel. These loafers were a '60s Ivy classic. **GM**

Opposite: Billy Strayhorn wears a classic seersucker suit, it's the inevitable choice for the discerning musician when the temperature rises. Seersucker is cool—literally. If fabric is the essential component of a good suit or jacket, then seersucker is a summer essential, it's the cat's whiskers. The name seersucker is a Hindu corruption of a Persian phrase *shir shaker*, which translates as 'milk and sugar'. In the 1930s, Brooks Brothers sold seersucker suits for $15. The fact that the brothers elevated what was considered a utilitarian fabric from the Southern United States into standard-issue Ivy is worth a mention in dispatches. It was taken up immediately by university men, the country club fellows and jazz musicians. The Monterey and Newport jazz festivals of the '60s were awash with seersucker, worn both by performers and the audience. *Above:* Sporting a very comfortable tweed sports jacket while concentrating on some sheet music. **GM**

BILLY STRAYHORN

(1915–1967)

Known to friends and musicians as Sweet Pea, Strayhorn was Duke Ellington's right-hand man and secret weapon. He penned 'Lush Life' and 'Take the "A" Train', two stellar examples of the Great American Songbook, as well as many other pieces, including 'A Flower is a Lovesome Thing' and 'Lotus Blossom' with Ellington. Openly gay, through Ellington's patronage, Strayhorn was able to write, live, and love without any fear of judgment or conflict from others. He was heavily involved in the civil rights movement and also a friend of Martin Luther King. Talking at his funeral, Ellington described Strayhorn as demanding 'freedom of expression...[He] lived in what we consider the most important and moral of freedoms: freedom from hate, unconditionally; freedom from self-pity (even throughout all the pain and bad news); freedom from fear of possibly doing something that might help another more than it might himself; and freedom from the kind of pride that could make a man feel he was better than his brother or neighbor.' **JJ**

The Freedom Rider
Art Blakey & The Jazz Messengers

STEREO
THE FINEST IN JAZZ SINCE 1939
84156 BLUE NOTE

LEE MORGAN / WAYNE SHORTER / BOBBY TIMMONS / JYMIE MERRITT

Art Blakey

ABDULLAH IBN BUHAINA (1919–1990)

Like Dizzy, Art Blakey had a spiritual relationship with his music. He converted to Islam in 1947, and while he kept Art Blakey as his performance name, he changed his name to Abdullah Ibn Buhaina. His friends and other musicians knew him as Buhaina. His ever-changing roster of musicians, and the name of the band—the Jazz Messengers—were all informed by the intention to affect positive change through music. The band was like a finishing school for emerging talent; musicians like Bobby Timmons, Freddie Hubbard, Branford Marsalis, Wynton Marsalis, Joanne Brackeen, Terence Blanchard, and Keith Jarrett all did a stint as Messengers early in their careers. The *Freedom Rider* album features Lee Morgan, Wayne Shorter, Bobby Timmons, Jymie Merritt, and, of course, Blakey on drums. The title track, a seven-and-a-half-minute drum solo, was recorded three weeks after the first Freedom Ride in 1961. **JJ**

Opposite: This image is strangely reminiscent of the work in the '80s of the great New York photographer Jamel Shabazz and his book, *Back in the Days*, documenting the emergence of the city's hip-hop culture. This image from 1958 features *(left to right)* Jazz Messengers **JACKIE McLEAN (1931–2006), SAM DOCKERY (1929–2015),** Art Blakey, **BILL HARDMAN (1933–1990),** and **JIMMY 'SPANKY' DeBREST (1937–1973),** with an assortment of headgear, extreme weather parkas, and overcoats all befitting the Black Ivy look. **JJ**

During the early '60s a new sound emerged, soon to be labelled soul jazz. Steeped in gospel style melodies and call and response interplay with a sanctified, hymn-like rhythm, these songs embodied a kind of nostalgia for a past that never was, that Black audiences could relate to on a deep emotional level. Lee Morgan's 'The Sidewinder', Horace Silver's 'Song For My Father', and Cannonball Adderley's live version of 'Mercy, Mercy, Mercy!' were a perfect soundtrack for the time, as the sound and the themes of the songs resonated with the religious undertones of the civil rights movement. But, despite their huge popularity and unprecedented record sales, there was a naivety about these songs, critics said disparagingly, that made them unworthy of being taken seriously. What the critics felt most disconcerting was that jazz had become politicized, with the inference that this back-to-church inspired sound could only be performed by Black musicians. **JJ**

Left: A meeting of musical minds. **HORACE SILVER (1928–2014)** wears a fine Batik pattern button-down shirt *(left)* while **LOUIS HAYES (B.1937)** chooses a more formal multi-stripe shirt with a skinny tie *(right)*. *Opposite:* On the cover of his album, **LEE MORGAN (1938–1972)** favours a comfortable, quintessentially American short-sleeve button-down shirt. It's a good look. **GM**

Lee Morgan

SEXTET

STEREO
THE FINEST IN JAZZ SINCE 1939
83024 BLUE NOTE

Julian Priester
George Coleman
Harold Mabern
Walter Booker
Mickey Roker

There's always something special about sessions. Sure, the musicians are there to work, but it's also a chance to hang, to talk, to have a drink and a smoke and even dance, maybe...and through all of that, create some great music in the process. It's no surprise, then, that clothes are an integral part of any session. Not only is it likely that you'll be photographed by someone like Francis Wolff for the cover art, but also you'll be meeting friends, fellow musicians, some of whom you've not seen for a while. Who knows, you may even be making recording history during that session.

Distinctive shirt styles worn by *(left, clockwise from top left)* **JACK WILSON (1936–2007)**, **HANK MOBLEY (1930–1986)**, **HERBIE HANCOCK (B.1940)** and Bobby Hutcherson *(see p.64)*, and *(above)* resplendent in short-sleeve button-down and cravat, Art Blakey. **JJ**

They say the US hat industry took a nose dive when John F. Kennedy became president. His aversion to hats, according to many, set a trend throughout the country, making not wearing one a thing. His impact on the hat industry was so immense that major hat manufacturers such as the Consolidated Millinery Co. and Hat Corp. of America sent him letters begging him to start wearing hats and prevent what they saw as an existential threat to their businesses. News of the hats' demise never seemed to reach the Black Ivy generation, especially jazz musicians. When it came to matters of the hat, they just kept on keeping on. Almost no hat was off limits in the Black Ivy wardrobe, from berets, to trilbies, to pork pie, and the beaver...everything except, maybe, the Davy Crockett, that is. Pictured here are *(opposite)*

DOUG WATKINS (1934–1962), *(above, clockwise from top left)* JOE HENDERSON (1937–2001), LOU DONALDSON (B.1926), WOODY SHAW (1944–1989), and FREDDIE ROACH (1931–1980). JJ

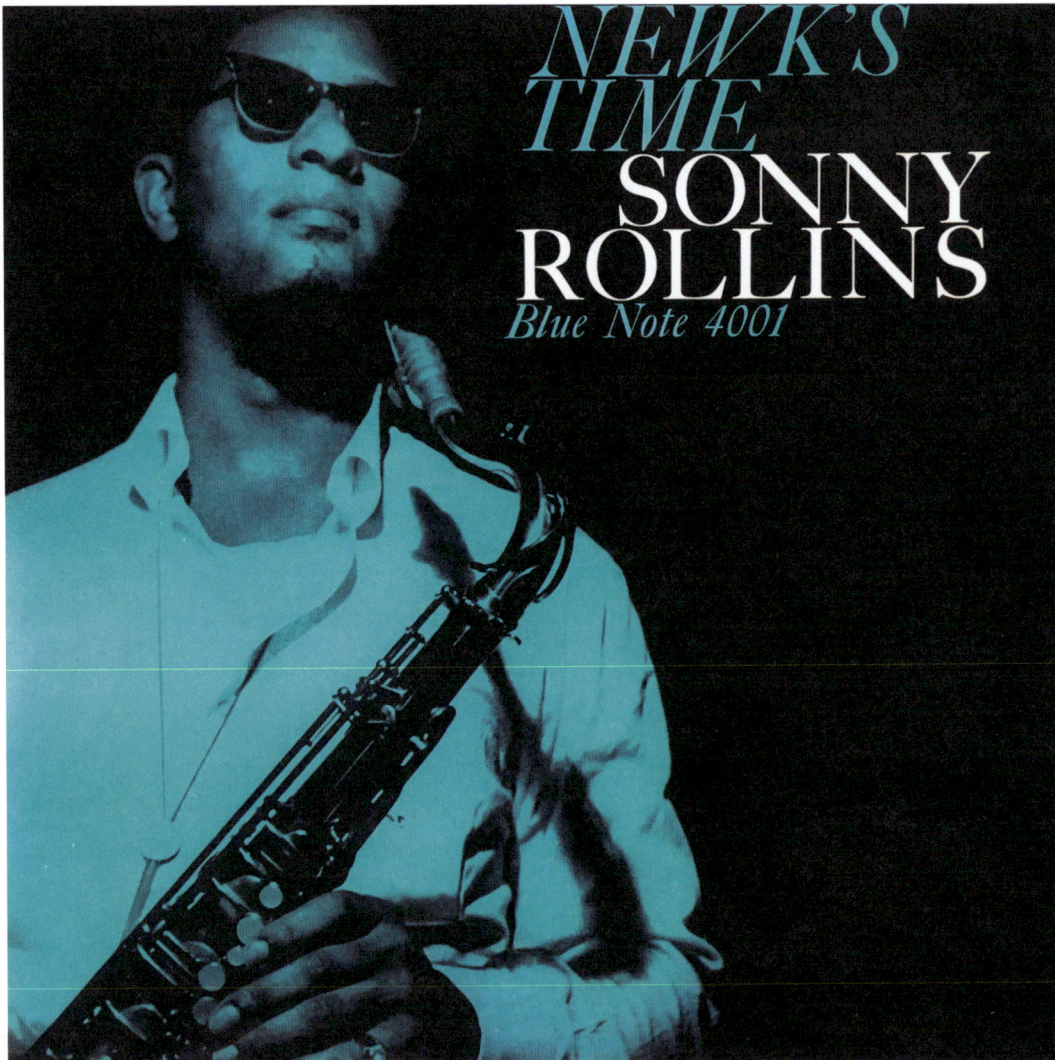

NEWK'S
TIME
SONNY
ROLLINS
Blue Note 4001

Sonny Rollins

(B.1930)

When tenor saxophonist Sonny Rollins walked up E 126th Street in Harlem on the morning of August 12, 1958, he wasn't just repping himself. Like the other prominent musicians there, he'd been invited to take part in a group portrait for *Esquire* magazine. It was a photo shoot by a rookie 32-year-old photographer called Art Kane for a piece in the magazine called *Harlem 1958*. Today, it is known as one of the most famous jazz photographs of all time. The story of the making of this now-iconic photograph was turned into an Oscar-nominated documentary in 1994, called *A Great Day in Harlem*. Since jazz musicians tended to live a nocturnal existence, it's hard to imagine seeing one, let alone in excess of 50, hanging out together on a Tuesday morning. But there they were, all fixed up, looking sharp and ready for their collective close-up. **JJ**

Opposite: When it came to clothing, followed by the epic roll on the collar on his button-down shirt, the curve at the front of his jacket was one of the most important things that distinguished Rollins from almost all the other musicians in attendance. Called a three-roll-two lapel, the top button detailing is intended for decorative purposes only. Today it's become a standard feature on almost all decent three-button suits. Regarded as a sign of sartorial sophistication, it dates back to the Ivy League campuses of the 1920s, and by the late '50s had become a traditional element of the Ivy dress code. By wearing a suit that looks distinctly like the classic Brooks Brothers hopsack, Rollins identified himself as part of an emerging idea, and aligned himself to a movement still in its infancy. Of course, like most of the sartorial rules seen as sacred by the Ivy establishment, this three-roll-two rule would quickly be bent, broken, and often tossed out altogether, as in the following decade Rollins and his generation co-opted the look and made the clothing their own. **JJ**

Left: This Blue Note album, *Newk's Time* (1959) by saxophone colossus Rollins, was photographed by the peerless Francis Wolff. Rollins wears a white button-down shirt with a perfect roll to the collar. **GM**

In a 2008 article, legendary British jazz multi-instrumentalist Orphy Robinson MBE described **CECIL TAYLOR (1929–2018)**, then 78, as 'Effortlessly stylish, in a Yohji Yamamoto kind of way'. A pioneer of the free jazz movement and with a dress sense as forward-looking as his music, Taylor accrued a huge and almost cult-like following of fans, despite the intrinsically complex nature of his music. **JJ**

This image represents the perfect combination. An excellent Dennis Stock photograph of a relaxed Cecil Taylor wearing a definitive blue university stripe button-down shirt, which was used on the cover of the 1959 album *The Cecil Taylor Quartet: Looking Ahead!*. Doesn't get much better, file under hip. **GM**

IN FILM

SCRIPTING THE FLIP

Sidney Poitier

(B.1927)

In 1999, the American Film Institute produced the *100 Years 100 Stars* list, featuring actors they considered to be Hollywood's greatest screen legends. While the likes of Steve McQueen, Montgomery Clift, Rudy Valentino, and Sir Alec Guinness never made the cut, among the 25 male stars was Sidney Poitier. Polling at number 22, not only was he the only living actor on the list, he was the only Black actor on the list.

Poitier's breakthrough role came in 1955 in *Blackboard Jungle,* playing a cocky adolescent in a poor inner-city school for boys. Way more intelligent than his fellow classmates, it becomes evident that he has little to no hope of escaping the same life of crime, violence, and poverty as everyone else. A sympathetic, even heroic character, it presented the African American as a victim of his environment. Fast forward to 1967 and the tables have turned. Now it's his turn to stand in front of the blackboard and wear the sports jacket with patch pocket and repp tie. In *To Sir, with Love,* based on the autobiography of writer E. R. Braithwaite, he plays a teacher newly arrived at a poor, inner-city secondary school in the east end of London. Here, refusing to allow himself or them to be victims of their environment, he elects to teach his pupils like adults, giving them life lessons in dignity, respect, and tolerance. In that same year he starred in two more films, *Guess Who's Coming to Dinner* and *In The Heat of the Night,* where he also presents the notion of nobility and dignity, and the need for the white characters in these stories, despite differences, to respect him for these qualities.

Being seen for one's humanity and recognised as equal was, of course, among the core goals of the civil rights movement, so it made perfect sense that Poitier's style of dress be an elegant reflection of Black Ivy style both on screen and off. **JJ**

Opposite: Wearing the perfect Ivy jacket complete with patch top pocket and repp tie in the film *To Sir, with Love* (1967). **GM**

Opposite: Sydney Pollack's movie directing debut was *The Slender Thread* (1965), starring Sidney Poitier and Anne Bancroft. Here on location, Sydney P, with megaphone, directs the other Sidney P; he's the one wearing the perfect corduroy jacket complete with elbow patches and 'old school' bicycle accessory. *Right:* This short-sleeve popover shirt with an unbuttoned collar, worn with a t-shirt underneath, looks about as good as it gets. **GM**

THEY WON'T STAY DEAD!

An IMAGE TEN Production

NIGHT OF THE LIVING DEAD

They keep coming back in a bloodthirsty lust for HUMAN FLESH!...

Pits the dead against the living in a struggle for survival!

Starring JUDITH O'DEA · DUANE JONES · MARILYN EASTMAN · KARL HARDMAN · JUDITH RIDLEY · KEITH WAYNE

Produced by Russel W. Streiner and Karl Hardman · Directed by George A. Romero · Screenplay by John A. Russo · A Walter Reade Organization Presentation — Released by Continental

Although its place in Black culture had already been secured by Public Enemy's song about the 1980s crack cocaine epidemic, *Night Of The Living Baseheads*, the film *Night Of The Living Dead* received something of a revival more recently with comparisons to Jordan Peele's award-winning film, *Get Out* (2017). *Living Dead* was released in 1968 and to the surprise of its makers and stars, the low budget, independent horror movie became an instant box office success, changing the horror movie genre forever. Directed by George A. Romero, it's considered by many as among one of the best films of the twentieth century. With its sparse locations, one-take scenes, and almost documentary-like cinematography, there's an immediacy about this film that makes it genuinely scary, even by contemporary standards. One factor that made the film's success even more surprising was that its lead role was played by Black actor **DUANE JONES** (1937–1988). According to Romero, although the role was originally written for a white character, Jones got the gig simply because he gave the best audition. This made him the only non-white character in the whole film. Romero denies any underlying social or political themes, but one can't help watch the drama unfold and—as with *Get Out*—reflect on the undercurrent of racial fear in the US and the similarities between the apocalyptic scenes in the film and actual TV news footage of police and home guard attacks on civil rights protestors, the Watts Riots, and others that took place after the killing of Martin Luther King, Jr. JJ

DELL 12c
12-526-810
OCTOBER

MISSION: IMPOSSIBLE

PETER GRAVES

MARTIN LANDAU

BARBARA BAIN

GREG MORRIS

PETER LUPUS

A STOLEN AIRLINER! TO DEFEAT A DICTATOR!

© 1968 PARAMOUNT PICTURES CORP. ALL RIGHTS RESERVED

Actor **GREG MORRIS** (1933–1996) played Barney Collier in the original TV series *Mission: Impossible*. Kind of like the character Q in the James Bond franchise, only a bit more pro-active, he was the team's technical wizard. His backstory had him as the president of Collier Electronics, a prized NASA contractor. Other TV roles played by Black actors at the time included Bill Cosby as tennis coach and US spy, Alexander Scott, in *I Spy*, and Don Mitchell as ex-con now live-in carer, Mark Sanger, in *Ironside*. What distinguished Morris' character from the others is that he wasn't ascribed a subservient role in the series, rather he was portrayed as an equal member of the Impossible Mission Force team. JJ

Dutchman is the last work Amiri Baraka penned under the name LeRoi Jones—from that point on he regards it as a slave name. Written in 1964, when mixed marriages were still illegal, and when Black men were summarily beaten or killed in the South for even being suspected of looking at a white woman, *Dutchman* begins with a white woman locking eyes with a young Black man on the platform of an otherwise deserted New York subway station. At one point she goads him, saying, 'Three-button suit! What right do you have to be wearing a three-button suit? Your grandfather was a slave, he didn't go to Harvard!' The play co-won an Off-Broadway Theatre Award in 1965 and was developed into a movie a year later.

These British film posters for *Dutchman* and *The Connection* were designed by one of Britain's most important post-war poster designers, Peter Strausfeld, for the Academy Cinema on London's Oxford Street. JJ

Over 20 top Critics say
'BRILLIANT'

THE CONNECTION (X)

Story JACK GELBER

Direction SHIRLEY CLARKE

MEN HELD CAPTIVE BY THE POWER OF DRUGS

Directed by Shirley Clarke, *The Cool World* is a kind of modernist, gothic, rights-of-passage movie, shot in the *cinema verité* style that was perfected by the French New Wave, and in turn inspired the likes of John Cassavetes, Albert and David Maysles, and much of Clarke's own work. Adapted by Clarke and her then partner, Carl Lee, who also plays one of the film's leads, it was made in 1963 and tells the story of a young Harlem gang and the desire of its members to get out. It's violent, pithy, realistic, and tragic. And the clothes are all a rugged, working class Black Ivy style. As a result, it's now regarded as a cult classic among true modernists.

The soundtrack boasts an original score composed by Mal Waldron, himself a major exponent of Black Ivy at the time. It's performed by Dizzy Gillespie—also no slouch when it came to sartorial matters. The novel, by white author Warren Miller, was published in 1960 and captures the moral panic centred around teenage delinquency, a nationwide fear that informed a whole slew of books and films around the time, including *Rebel Without a Cause* (1955), *Blackboard Jungle* (1955) and even *Westside Story* (1961).

Miller was an astute and insightful outsider who's work, although very much of its time, distilled an aspect of inner city youth culture that continues to resonate today. **JJ**

HOOKER!

FUZZ!

JUNK!

RUMBLE!

These are words that mean big trouble in

These are the ones who play it cool, and find out about life and love before they're in high school! This is the picture that explodes like a time bomb In the face of a city!

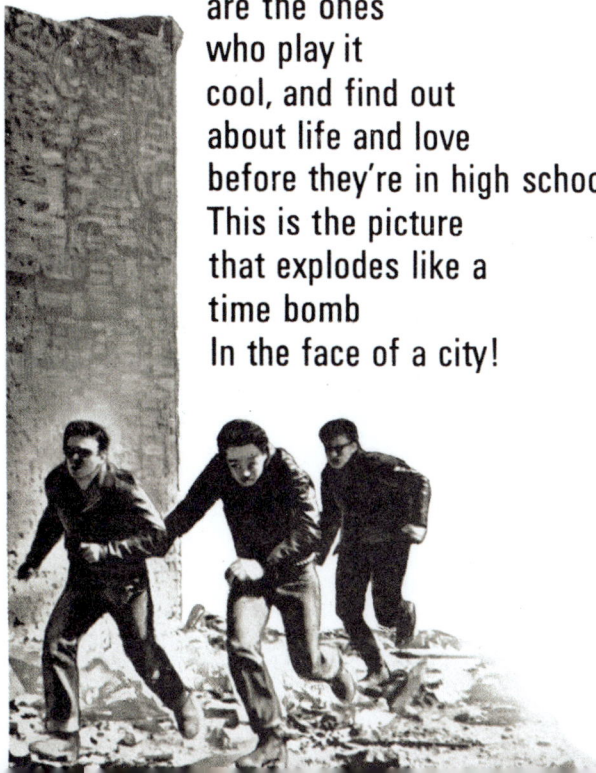

The Cool World

DIRECTED BY SHIRLEY CLARKE
PRODUCED BY FREDERICK WISEMAN
MUSIC BY MAL WALDRON
FEATURING DIZZY GILLESPIE

A CINEMA V PRESENTATION

IN SCHOOLS

LESSONS IN STYLE

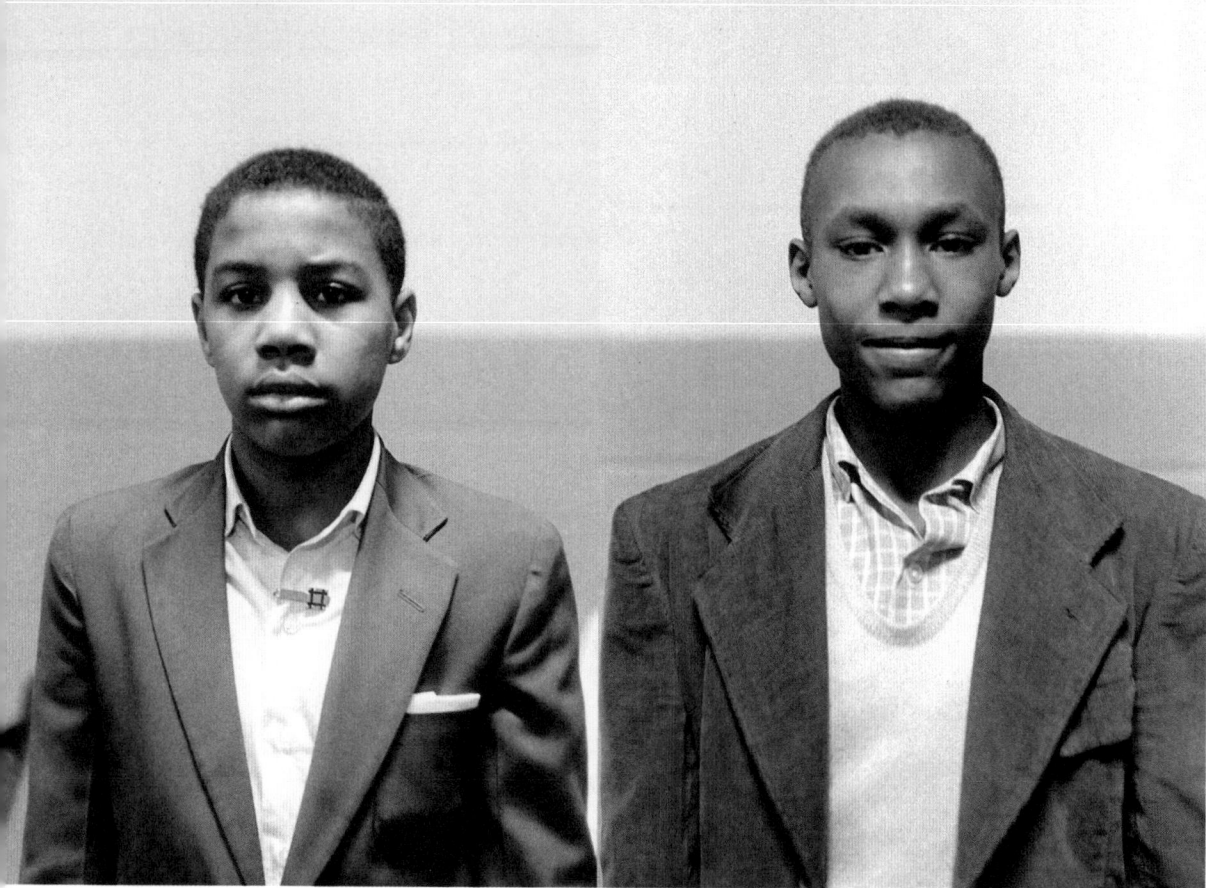

This is when kids became rule breakers and heroes at the same time. Here are some of the 'Norfolk 17' integrating previously all-white high schools in Norfolk, Virginia, in 1959. *Left: (clockwise from top left)* **ANDREW HEIDELBERG, FREDDY GONSOULAND, REGINALD YOUNG, EDWARD JORDAN,** and *opposite:* **LOUIS COUSINS.** On the first day at any school, you want to make a good impression. Although no matter what these kids wore, you can be pretty certain that, overall, their welcome was anything but enthusiastic. Despite that, there they are in their Black Ivy best, a tie here, a pocket square there, and over there, a slightly oversized corduroy jacket borrowed from an older brother. The windbreaker jacket, an Ivy and golfer staple, with its piped pocket outline and button cuff, is not dissimilar to the much-discussed cherry red windbreaker worn by James Dean in *Rebel Without a Cause.* Dean's was made by Bud Berma. This one looks distinctly like the classic Drizzler jacket by McGregor. In *Rebel*, Dean also played the new kid in school, a complete outsider, a disruptive influence on the classroom's status quo. However, unlike Dean's character who was a loner, these kids were the vanguard of a movement. As Public Enemy would say, theirs was a generation of rebels without a pause and it would take a nation of millions to hold them back. **JJ**

Newly enrolled in Maury High School in Norfolk, Virginia, a previously all-white school, fifteen-year-old Louis Cousins, still in his McGregor windbreaker, wears a V-neck sweater and plaid camp-collar shirt *(above)*, and a short collar button-down shirt, also plaid *(opposite)*. **JJ**

HAMILTON E. HOLMES (1941–1995) taking time out in his off-campus digs in 1961. Dressed in a shawl collar cardigan, button-down shirt, and desert boots, the goal of Black Ivists wasn't simply to subvert the style, it was also to subvert the institutions that gave rise to the style itself. **JJ**

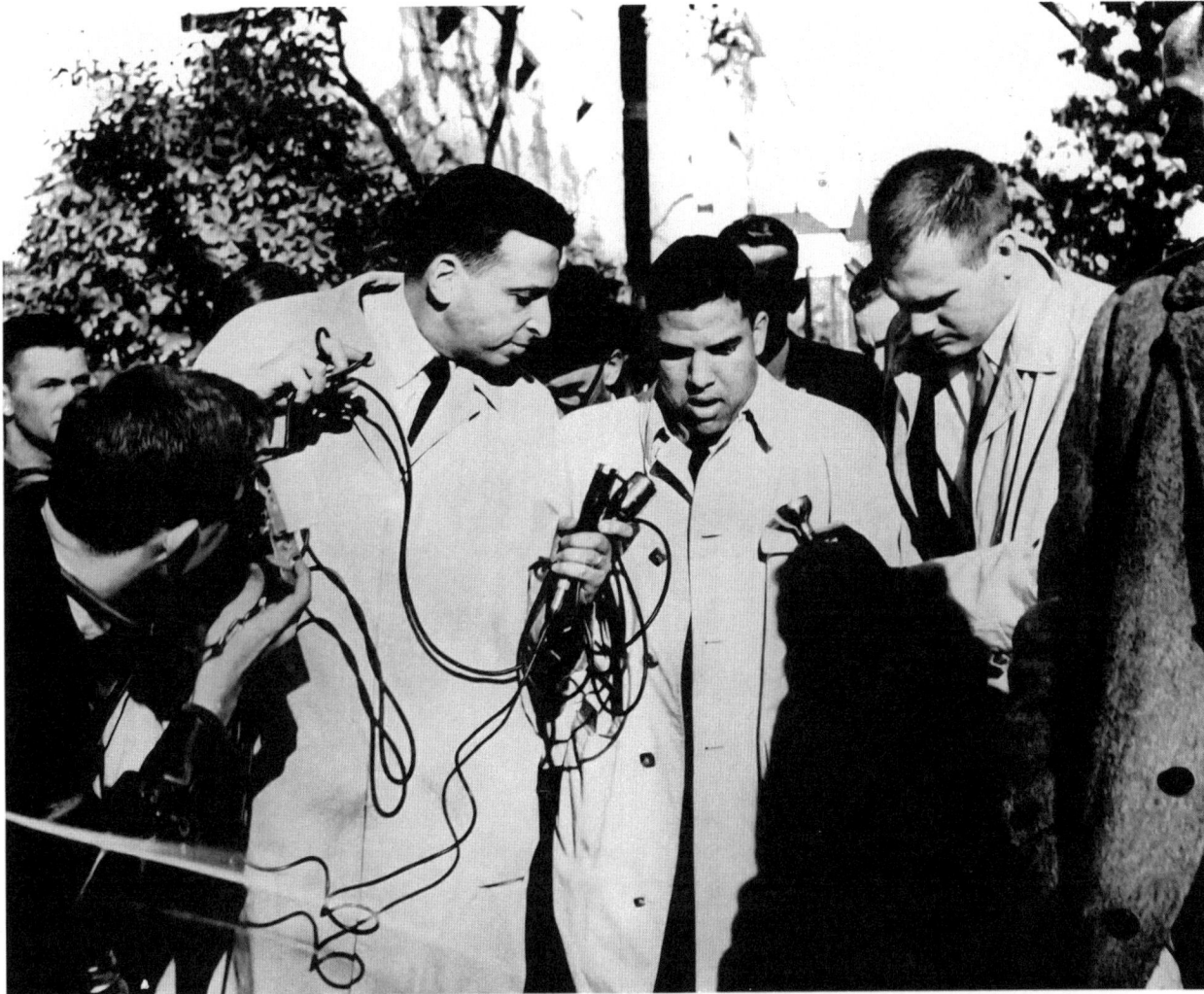

Besieged by reporters and photographers following his arrival on University of Georgia campus at Athens in January of 1961, Hamilton Holmes affirms his right to attend tax-maintained state institution. Holmes is now enrolled as a first year medical student at Emory University in Atlanta. He quietly integrated Emory in mid September.

THE LONELY YEARS OF HAMILTON HOLMES

Perseverance of University of Georgia race pioneer triumphs over insults and threats

BY ALAN WEXLER

IT WAS graduation day at the University of Georgia.

Silently, 21-year-old Hamilton Holmes took his place among some 1,600 graduates in the stands of majestic Sanford Stadium. His presence was barely noticeable amidst the sea of caps and gowns.

Few heads turned as he rose proudly when honor graduates of his College of Arts and Sciences were recognized. But to Holmes, this moment meant more than mere scholastic honor; it was the realization of his goals, his reward for more than two years of hard work and seemingly endless hours of self discipline and determination.

As the shadows of evening engulfed the field, he and the other members of the class of 1963 began their slow processional to receive their diplomas. There they split up, going to the various tables where their college deans stood, waiting to present degrees.

"The line came by, he walked up to me, I handed him his diploma, and then we shook hands," Dean Edison said afterwards. "There was nothing especially unusual about it."

Thus it was in this simple manner Hamilton Holmes became one of the first two Negroes to be graduated from the University of Georgia. Charlayne Hunter, the second Negro, received her degree in journalism at another part of the field.

Holmes walked away a *cum laude* graduate, a member of Phi Beta Kappa and Phi Kappa Phi honorary fraternities, and the recipient of a $1,200 yearly medical scholarship, which he is now using as Emory University's first Negro medical student.

His departure, as with Miss Hunter, was in stark contrast to his arrival in January, 1961. Student unrest at that time had culminated in a riot. However, after peace had been restored, things changed outwardly. Most students ignored them. Holmes had to live alone.

> The author of this article, Alan Wexler, is a member of Holmes' graduating class at the University of Georgia. Georgia-born and bred like Holmes, Wexler was a close observer of the young Negro student's ordeal from the latter's tumultuous arrival on campus in 1961 until his recent graduation.

You're looking at a future mayor of Charlotte, South Carolina, **HARVEY GANTT (B.1943)**, pictured here in a classic raglan sleeve overcoat worn over a blazer, undersize trilby hat, and shirt and tie combo. Note Gantt's immaculately processed hairstyle. There has been much discussion about Afro hair over the years, and although Black Ivy and the civil rights movement were not known for a particular style distinct from those worn generally at the time, perhaps the most popular was the natural hair cut, with etched-in parting, as worn by the likes of Bobby Timmons. Many say this hairstyle was the inspiration for modernist styles in the UK and beyond.

Studying architecture, Gantt was the first African-American student to be admitted to Clemson University. He later went on to MIT and then established his own architectural firm in Charlotte where, 20 years after he walked through those university doors, he became mayor. His achievement is exceptional, but he's not an exception. Many young Black students—both male and female—who through sheer force of will and legislation found themselves in previously segregated schools and colleges, went on to make huge contributions to society as a direct result of having seized that opportunity created by the Brown v. Board of Education decision in 1954, which declared segregated schools unconstitutional. **JJ**

There are Ivy League colleges and there are Black Ivy League colleges, historically the most prestigious of them being Morehouse, Howard, and the women's college Spelman. These and other Historically Black Universities And Colleges (HBUCs) can count some of America's most influential Black figures as alumni, then and now. They can also lay claim to championing the style of dress combining traditional Ivy with elements of jazz and street style to create something totally authentic, and that looks more contemporary than their establishment counterparts do today. JJ

MEN OF MOREHOUSE

Atlanta liberal arts college has produced large number of outstanding leaders

BY LERONE BENNETT Jr.

BOOKS and buildings do not make a great college. What counts most, said Cardinal Newman, is an atmosphere. Morehouse College, a school for men in Atlanta, Ga., is famous for its atmosphere. Benjamin Brawley, the college historian, called it an atmosphere of freedom. Benjamin Mays, the college president, calls it a "climate of expectancy."

This atmosphere has turned thousands of awkward youth into confident men and has made Morehouse one of the country's top liberal arts colleges. In a recent survey by Dr. Charles Thompson, dean of the Howard University Graduate School, Morehouse topped 82 Negro colleges in the percentage of doctorates on the faculty (47.7%) and the number of graduates who earned the Ph.D. degree between 1936-1956

(56). Morehouse also outranked 100 of 109 southern white private and church-related colleges in the first category and 102 of the 109 in the second category. Among the white colleges outdistanced by the Atlanta school were Florida Southern, Mercer (Georgia), Spring Hill (Alabama) and Millsap (Mississippi).

Morehouse Men say the college's reputation is no accident. They contend that a Morehouse education has a way of doing something special to its recipients. The record of achievement of Morehouse graduates lends weight to this argument. The school, which is sometimes called The College of Presidents, has produced leaders for 18 educational institutions. Nine Morehouse Men, including James M.

$$X_0 \mid X_{-1}, X_{-2}, \cdots \cdots).$$

$$\text{of the} \qquad \text{ss} \quad \{X_n\}$$

$$i \qquad , X_n)$$

um.

Left: Mathematics giant **DAVID BLACKWELL (1919–2010)** looking every bit the classic college professor teaching at the University of California in 1963. In 1955 he became the first Black faculty member there to gain full tenure. Blackwell had applied years earlier for a postdoc position at UOC. Back then he was interviewed by, and received a full endorsement from, statistician Jerzy Neyman. However, the head of the Math Department objected to the appointment because it was customary for professors to meet at each others' homes for dinner and, he explained, his wife 'was not going to have any darkie in her house'.

Blackwell's work has had a major impact on mathematics and statistics in the twentieth century. His research has led to major breakthroughs in the fields of Bayesian statistics, probability, information theory, game theory, and as the co-author of the Roa-Blackwell theorum, among others. Despite constant barriers, Blackwell also independently invented dynamic programming, a system now used in finance and applied to several areas of science, including genome analysis. *Opposite:* The progress and impact of the anti-segregation movement can be seen here in living colour, as an African-American lecturer conducts a business class of mixed students in Atlanta in 1968. The legacy of Black Ivy style is also on the money. **JJ**

IN THE CITY

FRESH LOOKS, FAMILIAR SCENES

As shocking and horrific as it is, the story of these two young Californians is only too familiar. Left is **RONALD FRYE (dates unknown)** and right is his brother **MARQUETTE FRYE (1944–1986)**, aged 21. On August 11, 1965, they were involved in an incident that resulted in the death of 35 people, 4,000 arrests, over 1,000 people injured, and the destruction of $40 million worth of property in what added up to six days of rioting in an otherwise ordinary, predominantly African-American neighbourhood in south LA. Stopped by a California Highway Patrolman, Marquette was suspected of driving while drunk. It was a Wednesday, a hot summer afternoon, and very soon a crowd gathered to watch the scene unfold. The boys' mother soon arrived to see her boys being forcibly arrested. Reports say that, attempting to protect her sons during the struggle, she tore one of the officer's shirts. One of the officers struck Marquette's head with a nightstick, then the police arrested the mother along with the two young men. This instance of police brutality outraged the few hundred onlookers, and triggered what became known as the Watts Riots. This photograph was taken a fortnight later as the brothers attended court for sentencing. Four months after the riots, the findings of an official government enquiry stated that the riots were triggered by a culmination of Black residents' longstanding dissatisfaction with high unemployment, poor housing and inadequate schools. **JJ**

In the summer of 1965, the police and the National Guard stamped out the Watts Riots, imposing curfews, emergency arrest powers, and extreme force. Stopped by a California Highway Patrol officer, these typical Watts kids look cool with their individual style—combining sportswear, tailoring, and customisation. Although the clothes look fresh, there's nothing unfamiliar about the scene itself. JJ

Bell-sleeved Alpaca cardigans, Catalina windbreaker jackets, caps, plaid shirts, and high-water Levi's with one-inch cuffs or turn-ups always hit the spot. Obviously, the desired look for these discerning young pilgrims was strictly Ivy. **GM**

The popularity of sunglasses here has a direct correlation to the beats and bebop generation. Wearing sunglasses—outdoors, indoors, during the day or night—showed a kind of detachment, if not disdain, for the outside world. The original Beats, a disaffected group looking for meaning in post-war, mid-century America, modelled themselves on Black jazz musicians like Charlie Parker, Dizzy Gillespie, and Lester Young. The most influential of the Beat writers, Jack Kerouac, often presented these musicians as sad, all-seeing, stoic characters in his work. In fact, much of the language Kerouac used in books such as *On the Road* and *The Dharma Bums*, words that were later adopted by hippies and ended up in the mainstream such as 'beat', 'cool', and 'hip', can be traced directly back to Lester Young and the coded terms he used to deflect attention from outsiders—in particular white people. Much like those words, back then, sunglasses were used to protect the wearer both literally and metaphorically. **JJ**

Left: Groove merchants. Our man is wearing double button-down. Not only has he got a button-down collar on his jacket but he is also sporting a button-down shirt with a superb roll on the collar, and to top it off a killer pair of shades. There is one particular Italian word that is overused but here is very apt—*sprezzatura*. **GM**

125

Young men gathering in a neighbourhood in Chicago as a group of local artists paint the legendary *Wall of Respect* in the summer of 1967. Here the mix of Ivy style and casual sportswear indicates streetwear looks of the future. **JJ**

IN CIVIL RIGHTS

WHO, WHAT...AND IF NOT NOW, WHEN?

Martin Luther King, Jr.

(1929–1968)

Although Martin Luther King, Jr. was committed to a policy of peaceful protest and direct action, it would be wrong to assume that he and the millions of other civil rights activists who followed him didn't retaliate. Instead of fighting violence with violence and prejudice with hate, they used the subversive force of style as their weapon of choice. That style created an epic cognitive dissonance among those who preferred to see African Americans as inferior and exhibit fear or rage in the face of abuse. Through this, King was able to garner the support of a wide variety of groups and push through change. From the 1955 Montgomery Bus Boycott, symbolized by Rosa Parkes, to the lunch counter sit-in in 1960, the Civil Rights Act of 1964, to the support of labour rights, the battle against voter suppression, and the challenge of the Vietnam War. Visually they were the embodiment of Black Ivy, from the pristine suits to the workwear and dungarees, to the khakis and pith helmets. But Black Ivy style isn't simply a way of dressing, it's a way of doing; as Michelle Obama once said, when they go low, we go high. **JJ**

Martin Luther King prepares to speak in Montgomery, Alabama, in 1965. While they appear to be his security detail, the fly front raglan sleeve raincoat—made popular by London Fog—and shades on the gentleman on the left, and the Prince of Wales check suit on the gentleman on the right mean they were also purveyors of Black Ivy. **JJ**

This is Martin Luther King, back in Atlanta University with a group of student activists, each of whom risked their lives and made enormous sacrifices for civil rights. The tie clips, the capped brogues, the collar pins, the suits, all take the idea of power dressing to another level. That's because the intention behind Black Ivy wasn't simply to dress like white college elites, it was, in part, to challenge racist stereotypes. In that respect, simply becoming visible as human beings was an essential part of the revolution. *Left:* King with Marion Barry. *Opposite: (from left, top row)* **BERNARD LEE (1935–1991), DAVID FORBES (B.1941), HENRY 'HANK' THOMAS (B.1941) LONNIE C. KING, JR. (1936–2019), JAMES LAWSON (B.1928);** *(middle row)* Virginius Bray Thornton III (*see p.148*), Wyatt Tee Walker (*see p.142*), Martin Luther King, Jr., **MICHAEL PENN (dates unknown);** *(bottom row)* **CLARENCE MITCHELL (1911–1984),** and Marion Barry (*see p.175*). **JJ**

Malcolm X

EL-HAJJ MALIK EL-SHABAZZ (1925–1965)

Malcolm X's journey took him from being a small-time, zoot suit-wearing Harlem hustler to the most notorious civil rights activist in America. As a leader in the Nation of Islam, he not only recruited thousands of new members and set up mosques throughout the US, he also became the face and voice of the movement, arguing that racial and economic equality could only be achieved through Black Nationalism and a separate state, establishing an agenda that would later be developed by the Black Panther Party and beyond.

When designing the costume for the 1992 Spike Lee biopic starring Denzel Washington, Avery Lucas said he was determined to capture 'that touch of flamboyance' that made Malcolm X's style so distinctive. A key part of his look was his glasses. Called Sirmont and made by American Optical, X owned a number of pairs all of the same model but made from different materials. This allowed him to change the frame according to what he was wearing at the time—now, if that isn't a touch of flamboyance, what is? JJ

Photographed here by legendary Magnum photographer Eve Arnold, X's pose is a fusion of elegance and defiance—in typical Black Ivy style—as the pin-sharp focus of the lens lands on his crescent moon and star clad hand. JJ

When it came to subverting the establishment dress codes, Malcolm X was way ahead of the game. The thing is, he looked so damn cool whatever he wore. **GM**

Left: In many ways the dress code of the Nation of Islam and that of the civil rights movement was possibly all the two groups had in common at the time. The Nation, or Black Muslims as the media liked to call them, were determined to elevate Black people in America with zero help from anyone else. *Opposite:* One of their greatest tools was the self published newspaper, *Muhammad Speaks*, which was founded by the Nation's Ministers, including Malcolm X, pictured here about to be distributed. JJ

The decline in popularity of the Black Ivy style began with the assassination of Martin Luther King and the emergence of the Black Panthers, and to a lesser degree the hippie movement. Dashikis and berets would replace button-downs and trilbies as the clothing of rebellion. Politicians such as SCLC leader **WALTER FAUNTROY (B.1933)**, photographed here *(left)* in 1968 while meeting with other civil rights activists after the assassination of Martin Luther King Jr., and *(right)* Congressman **ADAM CLAYTON POWELL, JR. (1908–1972)**, also photographed in 1968, were among the last to advance the style, and indeed their own idea of an integrated, civil society. **JJ**

Black Ivyists virtually weaponised sunglasses in this period, from the subterranean night life of Miles Davis at the Cafe Bohemia to the front line of civil rights activity, as in this photo *(left)* of civil rights leader **WYATT TEE WALKER (1928–2018)** in Birmingham, Alabama in 1963. Walker's super casual look with white t-shirt beneath the perfectly rolled Oxford button-down is a perfect contrast to *(right)* singer and civil rights activist **AL HIBBLER (1915–2001)** wearing a fiercely formal pinned, club collar shirt and tie. JJ

BOB MOSES (1935–2021) was the mild-mannered, almost zen-like mastermind behind the Freedom Summer of 1964: an epic voter registration drive that took place in the South's most committed segregationist state, Mississippi. Over 2,000 volunteers turned up, many of them white students from Ivy League schools, to help the Black population register to vote—confronting major resistance, bullying, intimidation, and also murder in the process. Rarely seen in a suit, what Moses displayed at the time was that clear leadership didn't have to come packaged in a suit and tie but could be just as effective in a popover shirt, needlecord trousers and Pro-Keds canvas sneakers. **JJ**

NEGRO PROGRESS IN 1960

Student sit-in demonstrators at Houston, Tex., cafeteria typify young Southern Negroes' newly emerged spirit of defiance against Dixie's tradition of racial injustice. Started early last year in Greensboro, N. C., sit-ins spread throughout South (except Mississippi) and were actively supported by sympathy protests in North, East and West.

Massive sit-in movement constitutes year's major step on road toward freedom

DESPITE the recent outbreaks of violence over public school integration in New Orleans, the collective gains made by Negroes in 1960 continued the trend of gradual progress in nearly all important phases of life. Foremost among these gains were those derived from the full-scale "sit-in" attack on Dixie lunch counter bias, which ushered in a new era of militant action by Southern Negro youth in behalf of racial equality.

Started on February 1 by four students in Greensboro, N. C., sit-ins spread rapidly throughout the South while attracting heavy support from white and Negro sympathizers in the rest of the country. The demonstrations' returns were substantial. Before the year had ended, four major variety store chains reported the desegregation of their lunch counters in 112 mostly Southern cities with promises of more to come. But outweighing these immediate gains in importance are the far-reaching effects of the reversal of Dixie's "massive resistance" as a new weapon against Southern bigotry.

As the year that spawned the first federal civil right legislation since Reconstruction, 1960 stands out in another area of Negro progress. Features of the controversial bill include a provision empowering federal judges to appoint referees in disputes arising from the denial of

Negroes' voting rights and requiring state election officials to retain voting records for 22 months for Justice Dept. probes. While some Negro rights specialists, including Thurgood Marshall, reject the bill as too cumbersome to be of much help, others have endorsed it as a positive, though meek, step in the right direction.

Advancements in civil rights on state and local levels were few and far between. They included the overruling of Arizona's anti-miscegenation statute by the State Superior Court, the creation of a Human Rights Commission by the Kentucky legislature, a New York law prohibiting insurance companies from charging racially discriminatory rates and a Kansas City, Mo., ordinance forbidding bias in hotels and restaurants.

A considerably brighter outlook was provided by the 1960 political arena in which the decisive victory of Tennessee's liberal encumbent Sen. Estes Kefauver over an avowed segregationist opponent set an encouraging trend. The trend continued with the adoption of the most liberal platforms in the two major parties' respective histories and an unprecedented wide use of Negroes as key presidential election campaigners by both camps. On Nov. 8, it reached its climax with the election of a President, irrevocably committed to the advancement of equality for all.

Sit-in protests began in Wichita, Kansas, in 1958, but the more famous sit-in, which many believe inspired the ones that followed, took place in Greensboro, North Carolina, in 1960, challenging segregated spaces such as hotels, clubs, and lunch counters. It's hard to imagine, especially in the face of staunch and often violent resistance, that such an approach could be so effective. But it was. Here a group of students wait to enter a segregated restaurant. JJ

Above: In short collar button-down and madras check jacket is **VIRGINIUS BRAY THORNTON III (1934–2015)**. Although he and his cohort of college demonstrators were expelled from college for their actions, he would soon afterwards go on to become a founding member of the Student Nonviolent Coordinating Committee (SNCC), one of the most important organizations within the civil rights movement. *Right:* Thornton leads a group of fellow students in full battle dress—hopsack summer-weight sports jackets, button-down shirts, and ties. Their destination? The whites-only lunch counter at Woolworth. **JJ**

Opposite: Thornton waits patiently to be served... or not, as the case may be.
Above: Non-reaction was the ultimate act of resistance. Each sitter had to undergo training to prep them for the experience. Being called the N-word, having liquid poured over them, or, as in this image of Thornton, cigarette smoke blown in their faces... would only be the tip of the attack they would come to experience in a real-life situation. **JJ**

African Americans have long been aware of their ability to effect change though their currency as consumers. *Left:* Combining peaceful protest with boycott power these images show civil rights activists calling for a boycott of Kresge—nowadays known better as Kmart—as a result of its discriminatory policies. One of the most impactful strategies of this kind was Operation Breadbasket, founded by Martin Luther King's Southern Christian Leadership Conference (SCLC) in Atlanta in 1962; 'Many retail businesses and consumer-goods industries deplete the ghetto by selling to Negroes without returning to the community any of the profits through fair hiring practices', said King. 'The fundamental premise of Breadbasket is a simple one. Negroes need not patronize a business which denies them jobs, or advancement [or] plain courtesy.' In typical Black Ivy style, although demanding people prioritise respect over retail, they ensured that they looked damned good while doing it. *Opposite:* A young man holds a placard highlighting the warped world of Jim Crow segregation, wearing a key piece in any Ivy wardrobe—a Harrington. This iconic jacket acquired its name in London when modernist menswear retailer John Simons sold his own version of the design and named it after 'Rodney Harrington', the character played by Ryan O'Neal in the TV series *Peyton Place*. **JJ**

You Can Buy a $50 SUIT But NOT a 10¢ CUP OF COFFEE

Taken in 1963 by Richard
Avedon, this image shows
JULIAN BOND (1940–2015)
standing in front of a group
of fellow activists. Bond
left Morehouse before his
final semester to become
a member of the SNCC. In
1965 he ran for the Georgia
State legislature with the
SNCC's support. Although he
won by a landslide, Bond was
denied his seat because he
opposed the Vietnam War.
So he campaigned again and
won again...and again. It was
after this third election victory
that a Supreme Court decision
made it possible for him to be
sworn in. He was 26. With this
in mind, his classic, seemingly
trad Ivy look, takes on a whole
different meaning. **JJ**

Bond is a young man who
buttons down his collars under
his Shetland crew
neck sweater and then
throws the perfect natural
shouldered Ivy jacket over
the whole outfit. **GM**

The spark that ignited the
Black Ivy style began to fade
with the death of Martin
Luther King in 1968. The
force of conviction, King's
dream, was based on the
belief that African Americans
could effect change in others
by being examples of that
change. When King died,
many lost faith in that idea,
some became completely
disillusioned, while others,
members of the Black Panther
Party, for example, became
even more determined. This
line is of mourners paying
respect to King as his body
lay in state at Spelman
College, Atlanta, ahead of
his funeral. JJ

IN MARCHES

THE PROTEST OF A PROUD MINORITY

MARCH ON WASHINGTON FOR JOBS AND FREEDOM
AUGUST 28, 1963

LINCOLN MEMORIAL PROGRAM

1.	The National Anthem	*Led by* Marian Anderson.
2.	Invocation	The Very Rev. Patrick O'Boyle, *Archbishop of Washington.*
3.	Opening Remarks	A. Philip Randolph, *Director March on Washington for Jobs and Freedom.*
4.	Remarks	Dr. Eugene Carson Blake, *Stated Clerk, United Presbyterian Church of the U.S.A.; Vice Chairman, Commission on Race Relations of the National Council of Churches of Christ in America.*
5.	Tribute to Negro Women Fighters for Freedom Daisy Bates Diane Nash Bevel Mrs. Medgar Evers Mrs. Herbert Lee Rosa Parks Gloria Richardson	Mrs. Medgar Evers
6.	Remarks	John Lewis, *National Chairman, Student Nonviolent Coordinating Committee.*
7.	Remarks	Walter Reuther, *President, United Automobile, Aerospace and Agricultural Implement Wokers of America; AFL-CIO; Chairman, Industrial Union Department, AFL-CIO.*
8.	Remarks	James Farmer, *National Director, Congress of Racial Equality.*
9.	Selection	Eva Jessye *Choir*
10.	Prayer	Rabbi Uri Miller, *President Synagogue Council of America.*
11.	Remarks	Whitney M. Young, Jr., *Executive Director, National Urban League.*
12.	Remarks	Mathew Ahmann, *Executive Director, National Catholic Conference for Interracial Justice.*
13.	Remarks	Roy Wilkins, *Executive Secretary, National Association for the Advancement of Colored People.*
14.	Selection	Miss Mahalia Jackson
15.	Remarks	Rabbi Joachim Prinz, *President American Jewish Congress.*
16.	Remarks	The Rev. Dr. Martin Luther King, Jr., *President, Southern Christian Leadership Conference.*
17.	The Pledge	A Philip Randolph
18.	Benediction	Dr. Benjamin E. Mays, *President, Morehouse College.*

"WE SHALL OVERCOME"

At The March on Washington for Jobs and Freedom in August 1963, the feeling of optimism and positivity on the day are almost palpable, as civil rights leaders pose for a historic photograph in front of the Lincoln Memorial. A pinnacle moment in the history of the civil rights campaign, it's where Martin Luther King gave his *I Have A Dream* speech. JJ

Above: Kids taking in the sights perched on the plinth of one of the Capitol monuments in Washington. *Opposite:* An NAACP supporter wears an unbuttoned tab collared shirt: this style is part of that never-knowingly-underdressed code that was inherent in the Black Ivy look. It was overtly neat and to the point of extreme, and while it tended to be worn by the mainstream in a formal business setting it was simply worn whenever within the Black Ivy community. The curved edge of the club collar, the snap tab or button tab fastening that elevated the tie and kept it in place showed a level of sophistication that to this day is off the chart. Its roots were firmly attached to the British upper classes, within the language of Black Ivy style this was an unequivocal 'so what' to the barriers of elitism. An expression of this attitude is to wear the shirt unfastened or fastened without a tie. **JJ**

Opposite: Marchers continue the message of peaceful protest. *Left:* Sidney Poitier and **HARRY BELAFONTE (B.1927)** await the speeches at the March on Washington. **JJ**

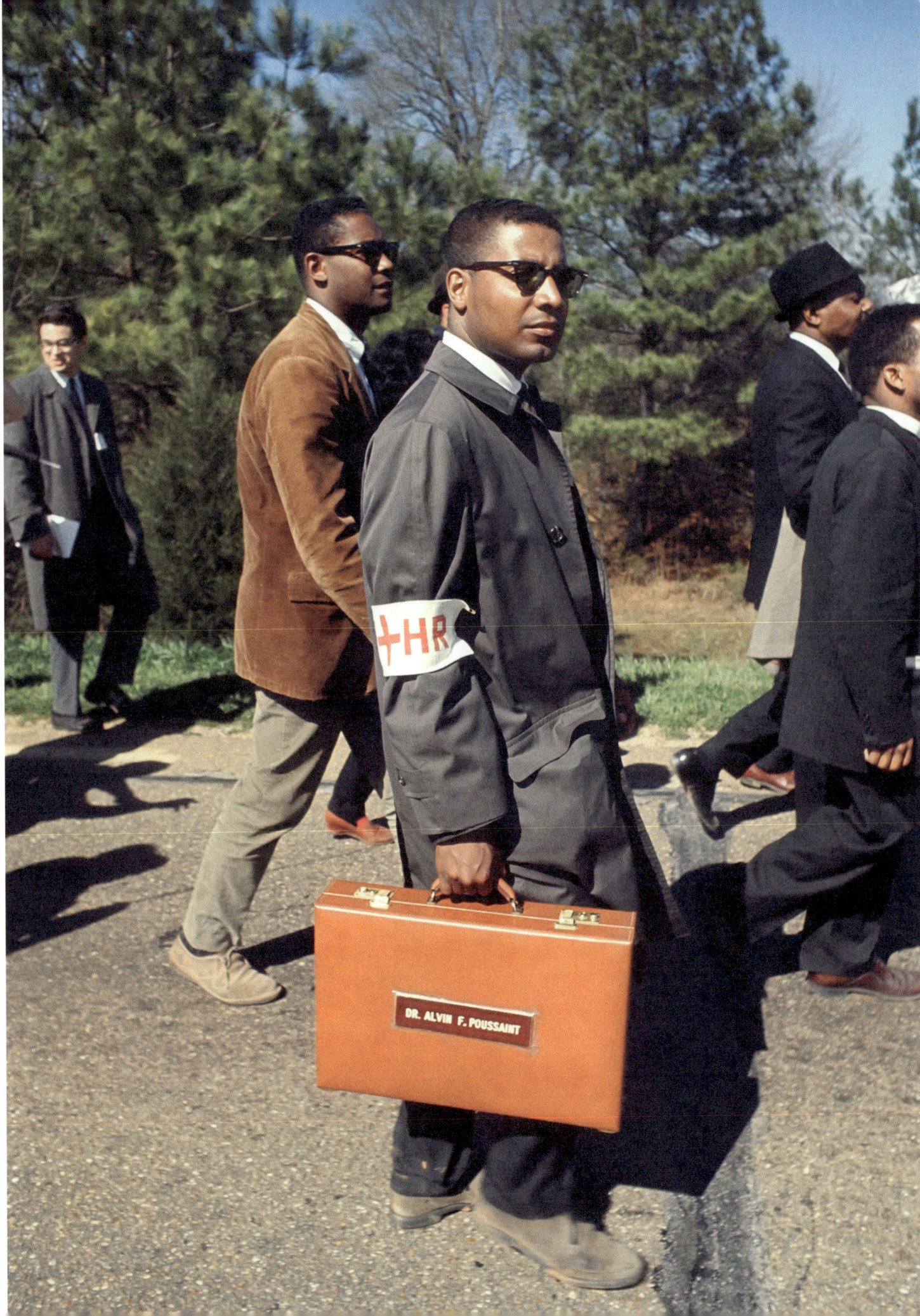

Opposite: It's a look you're more likely to be familiar with on the subway or the city streets, but here's **DR ALVIN F. POUSSAINT (B.1934),** a renowned psychiatrist famous for his work exploring the effects of racism on Black communities, marching from Selma to Montgomery in 1965. Over his suit, he's wearing a tonic coat, a jewel in any modernist wardrobe, then and now. *Right:* An iconic image from the Selma Montgomery marches on the cover of *Ebony* magazine; *(left to right)* **RALPH ABERNATHY (1926–1990), RUTH HARRIS BUNCHE (1906–1988), RALPH BUNCHE (1904–1971),** Martin Luther King, **CORETTA SCOTT KING (1927–2006). JJ**

EBONY

MY 30 YEARS WITH FATHER DIVINE:
Ex-member discusses money, love, sex and faith in religious cult
BY RUTH BOAZ

MARILYN SHOES

50,000 MARCH ON MONTGOMERY

MAY 1965 50c

Above: Three campaigners, including SNCC activist **EDDIE C. BROWN (1941–2011)**, dressed as elegantly as if he were going on a date, every detail considered, even the key line of his belt. *Opposite:* Facing adverse weather in consummate style—wearing suitably oversized macks and, of course, those all essential hats. **JJ**

Within the world of mainstream Ivy clothing, workwear doesn't make the grade. Rooted in the elite Ivy League schools, workwear—denim, chambray shirts, dungarees, chore coats and workboots—were an anathema. But within the Black Ivy wardrobe, it has pride of place. During the civil rights period, when activists from the Northern states went to the South to assist local branches of the SNCC and the Congress of Racial Equality (CORE) mobilize the local inhabitants' voting registration, it became obvious that wearing suits and ties while trying to gain the trust of local sharecroppers was not going to work. The elegant solution was to dress like the sharecroppers, not only by way of showing that they were prepared to help out with some farm work if it was required, but also demonstrating their support and solidarity to the outside world. By wearing these clothes they were saying yes, even farm workers in the remotest rural South have just as much right to vote, fair wages, and a decent education as anyone else in the United States. It was this that gave denim and workwear its rebellious image, the impact of which resulted in an industry-wide boom in the early '70s for companies like Levi's, Lee, and Wrangler, alongside others such as Maverick, and Big Smith. These companies, of course, worked very hard to reframe the narrative, making the jeans both cool and mainstream but casting the likes of James Dean, Marlon Brando, and the myth of the cowboy in the role of the denim-clad rebel. **JJ**

Opposite: Here's **C.T. VIVIAN (1924–2020)**, wearing a dog tooth raglan sleeve overcoat, fully buttoned to the neck, talking with a fellow activist during the marches between Selma and Montgomery. *Right:* **ANDREW YOUNG (B.1932)**, later to become the first African-American United States Ambassador to the United Nations, wearing an overcoat, turned up dungarees and moc toe workshoes, very similar to today's Red Wing 'Postman' shoe, originally designed in 1954. Both Young and Vivian were members of the Southern Christian Leadership Conference and worked closely with its president, Martin Luther King. **JJ**

In the foreground sits the future of denim, his approach that of the rebel. The disaffected would soon provide the template for denim wearers and denim makers to emulate worldwide. Unlike traditional Ivy style, Black Ivy aimed to honour the outsider. Sitting in the back booth at this sit-in protest in Atlanta are leading SNCC campaigners **COURTLAND COX (B.1941)** and **MARION BARRY (1936–2014). JJ**

Left: **A Steve Schapiro photograph of Martin Luther King linking arms with fellow marchers as a show of unity on the road from Selma to Montgomery in 1965. Left to right are Ralph Abernathy** *(see p.167),* **JAMES FORMAN (1928–2005), Martin Luther King, and JESSE DOUGLAS (B.1930).** *Opposite:* **An iconic image by Bruce Davidson of a marcher, looking as revelant today as he did then. The bib and brace overalls he is wearing are by Sanforized, a brand co-owned at the time by Sanford Lockwood Cluett, the inventor of Sanforization— a process that transformed the denim industry. His company, Cluett, Peabody & Co., was also responsible for Arrow shirts. JJ**

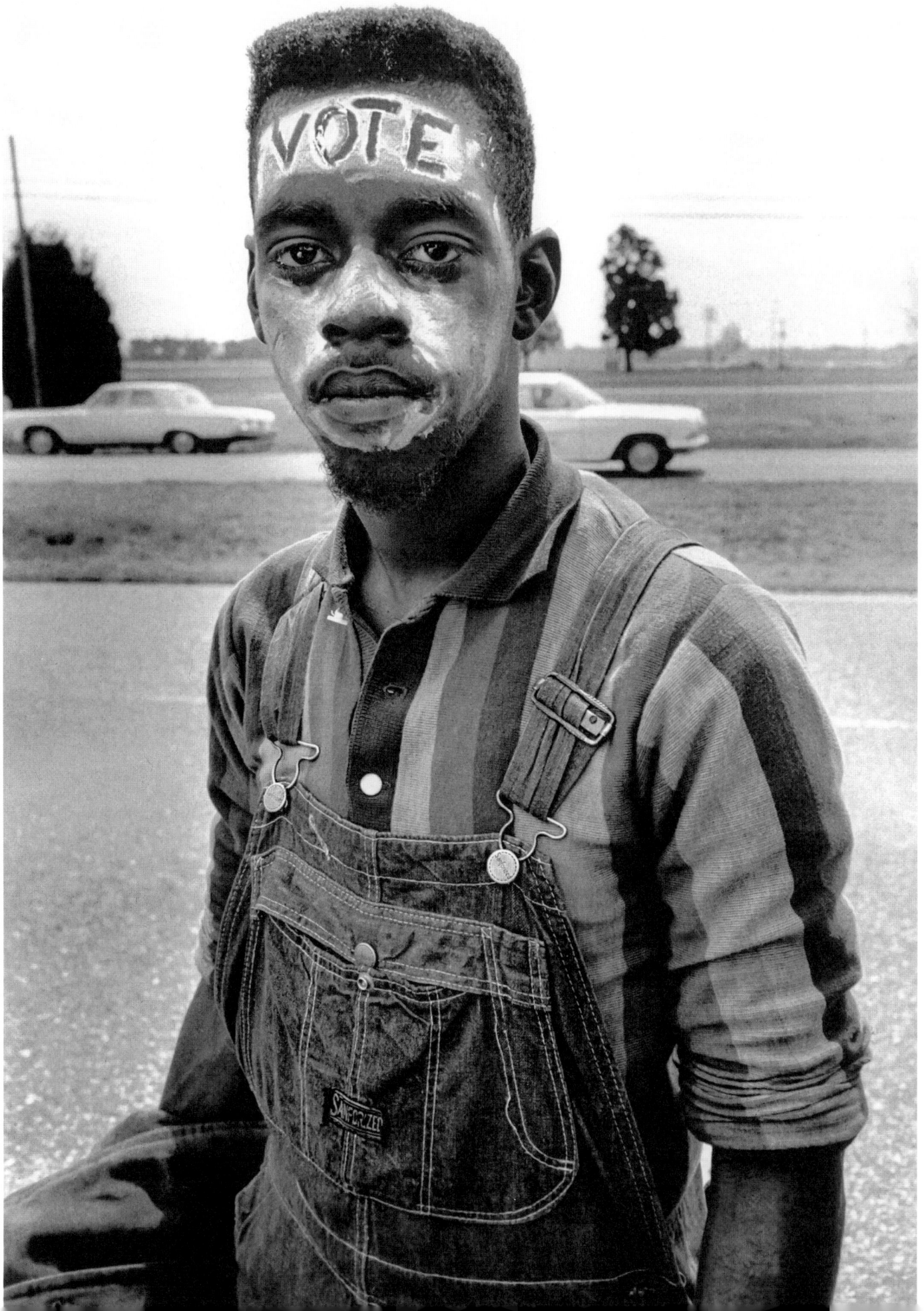

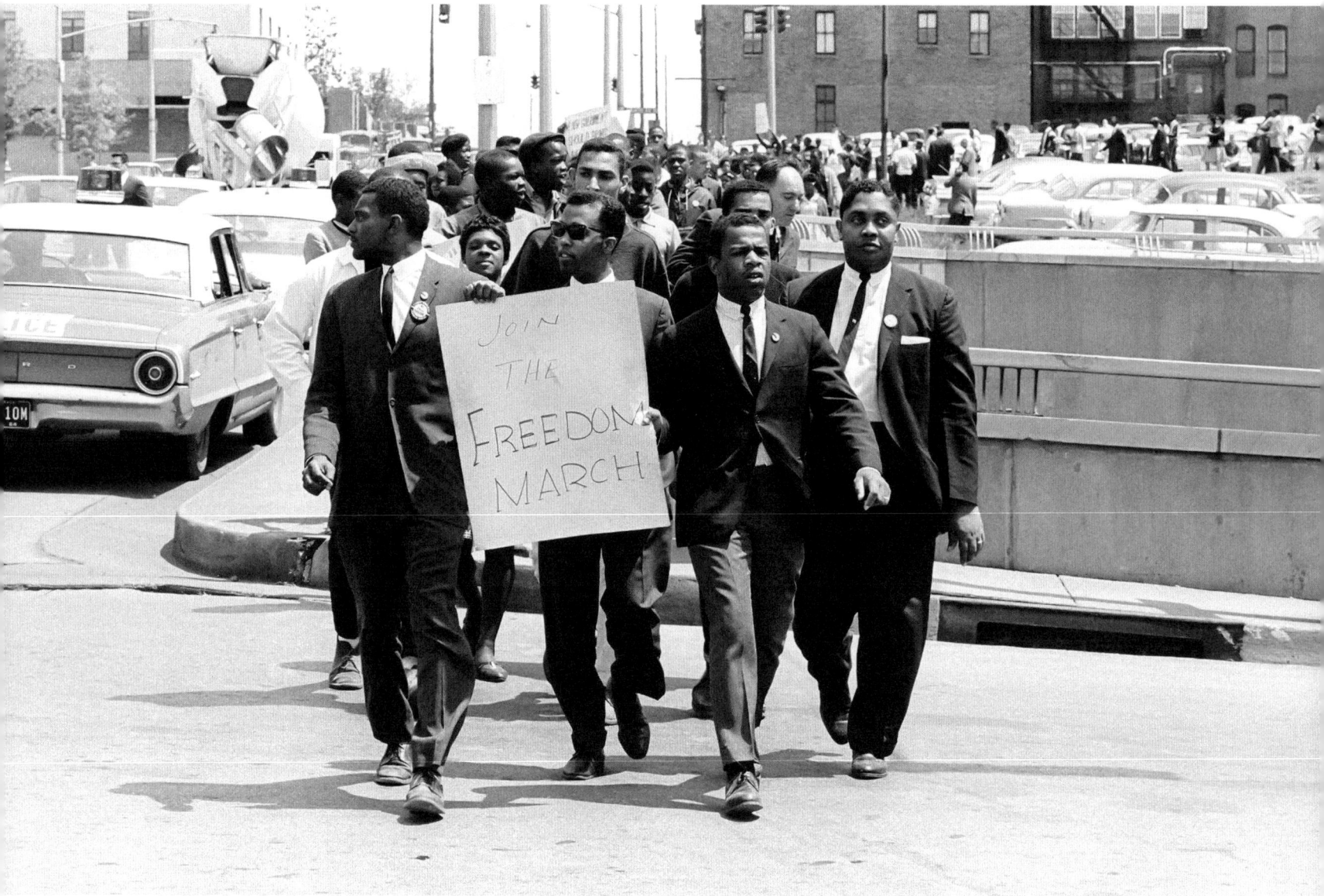

The conscience of Congress, **JOHN LEWIS (1940–2020)**, wearing his signature style of the period, tab collar shirt and tie, leads marchers through the streets. As chairman of the SNCC, he would be one of the Big Six who helped organize the epic March on Washington. **JJ**

178

It was images such as these, taken some 50 years ago, that inspired professional basketball players Colin Kaepernick and Eric Reid's silent protest on the sidelines during the playing of the US national anthem before the start of every game in 2016. Like the civil rights activists of the '60s, Kaepernick and Reid were calling for social justice and an end to the police brutality meted out on African Americans. *Opposite:* Martin Luther King leads a group of civil rights activists in Selma, Alabama, in prayer and protest in 1965 after a group of 250 protestors were arrested during a march to the Dallas County Courthouse as part of a voter registration drive. One of those praying alongside King is fellow civil rights leader Ralph Abernathy. *Above:* John Lewis, and others, takes the knee to demonstrate outside a Whites Only swimming pool in Cairo, Illinois. JJ

'Every new fashion is a form of rebellion.'
Sidney Poitier

The Black Ivyist had no qualms about raiding supposedly forbidden wardrobes in order to affirm their status as equal citizens. As a result, it not only encapsulated both workwear, sportswear, and Ivy League clothing, it also reframed western styling as well. Here's Sidney Poitier wearing shades and a western yoke windbreaker. Alongside him is Andrew Young, among others, all decked out in denim. Style-wise, this look is more evocative of the Buffalo Soldiers, the all-Black cavalry, and infantry regiments from the mid 1800s, than the traditional image of the cowboy. JJ

**STOKELY CARMICHAEL/
KWAME TURE (1941–1998)**
would later become Honorary
Prime Minister of the Black
Panther Party, and was
identified by the FBI as the
man most likely to succeed
Malcolm X. He's also the man
who popularized the term
Black Power. He initially came
to prominence as a leading
member of the SNCC, working
closely with Martin Luther
King and John Lewis. These
two images show Carmichael
in Black Ivy attire, the trench
coat, sports jacket, button-
down shirt, and tie on the
left, and beat work shirt and
denim on the right. Before
long, however, he would be
wearing dark glasses, a black
leather jacket, and carrying
a rifle. In 1966, following the
attack and hospitalization
of James Meredith,
Carmichael joined the March
Against Fear, only to be
arrested and jailed
in Greenwood. On his release
from prison, he made his
first Black Power speech,
essentially signaling the
end of the civil rights
experiment. **JJ**

The debate rages as to whether or not the open neck camp collar shirt has a place in the Ivy look wardrobe. But in the world of Black Ivy, it's the stuff of legend. To many African Americans it became a symbol of the kind of egalitarian lifestyle they were calling for. They, too, deserved to have access to the white picket fence, the two kids, and the security that they wouldn't be arrested or lynched for talking back to a white person. The consensus among civil rights leaders was that the key to attaining this was by leveraging the Black vote.

JAMES MEREDITH (B.1933) had a goal to walk through Mississippi and inspire the silent majority to get on the electoral register, regardless of the extremely hostile environment and the huge risks involved. He had already experienced the impact a solitary figure could have when he became the first African American to enrol in Mississippi State University. Here he is on day one of his trek, June 6, 1966, about to start his mammoth, heroic journey. By the end of day two, he was in hospital, his body riddled with injuries from three bullets from a buckshot rifle. This near-fatal incident had the effect of galvanizing civil rights' leaders into action. Up to that point, King had avoided the state, knowing that taking on the racism there was likely to result in total failure, or his assassination. Soon thousands of people would be walking the path planned by James, many of them, of course, dressed in Black Ivy, including camp collar style shirts worn over white t-shirts. **JJ**

IN POLITICS

LEADERS CUT FROM A DIFFERENT CLOTH

In 1960 **ANDREW HATCHER** (1923–1990) became the country's first Black press secretary to the White House, appointed by the newly elected President John F Kennedy. In addition to his press secretary duties, he advised the president on issues of race and civil rights. In 1963 he launched the organization 100 Black Men of America. Today, this civic organization, aimed at educating Black children and teens, has over 1,000 members with more than 11 chapters throughout the US. The organization recognizes that the visibility of successful African Americans has an immense impact on younger generations: one of its mottos is 'what they see is what they'll be'. Needless to say, Hatcher's personal style was impeccable. **JJ**

EDWARD WILLIAM BROOKE III (1919–2015) graduated from the Boston University School of Law. A member of the moderate, liberal wing of the Republican party, he went on to represent Massachusetts in the Senate between 1967 and 1979.

Brookes saw the civil rights leaders, such as Stokely Carmichael and others, as extremist—although on certain issues their views seem to coincide, including education and housing. Later in his career, Brookes would make history as the first

Republican leader to call for the then president, Richard Nixon, to resign following the infamous Saturday Night Massacre. Here is Brooke wearing a three-piece suit and repp tie. **JJ**

Opposite: It's August 1968, **CHANNING E. PHILLIPS (1928–1987)** is wearing a seersucker jacket. He becomes the first African American to receive votes for the presidential nomination at a Democratic National Convention. Phillips had been Robert F Kennedy's DC campaign manager, but following Kennedy's assassination in June '68, the DC delegation proposed that he run as Kennedy's replacement. Although he failed to get enough votes, of the candidacy Phillips said that it shows 'the Negro vote must not be taken for granted.' (*NY Times*, 1987).

Above: **CECIL F. POOLE (1914–1997)** at 46 and a Harvard law graduate as he is sworn in by Chief US District Judge, Louis E. Goodman, as US Attorney for the Northern District of California. Looking on are Poole's wife and two daughters, Gail, 14, and Patricia, 9. Before taking the bench, Poole was a law professor at UC Berkeley, director of NAACP Legal Defense and Educational Fund, and a trustee of the Urban League. Appointed by President Kennedy, Poole will handle the government's legal business in the Northern District of California, the nation's fourth largest. Poole's tenure was not without controversy, including preventing law enforcement from arresting members of the Black Panther Party who were conducting a peaceful protest in downtown San Francisco, and refusing to prosecute cases for Vietnam draft evasions unless there was a strong chance of conviction. **JJ**

IN SPORTS

GAMECHANGERS, MAVERICKS, AND REVOLUTIONARIES

The Oxford button-down
shirt. Talk to anyone about
Ivy style and it's likely
that the first thing they'll
mention is the Oxford
button-down shirt, an item
of clothing appropriated
from the British. While
Ivy League clothing, the
styles developed by Brooks
Brothers over 200 years
ago, lie at the core of
American menswear, its
own roots originate from
English universities and prep
schools. Originally invented
in Scotland and worn during
sports activities such as
polo in the early 1900s,
the key to a good Oxford
button-down is the wave
you get on the collar, this is
best achieved by wearing an
unlined, unfused shirt collar.
Left: Dressed in an Oxford
button-down, and Oxford
brogues, we see
**MUHAMMAD ALI
(1942–2016, THEN
CASSIUS MARCELLUS
CLAY, JR.)** the day after he
wins his first Heavyweight
Championship against Sonny
Liston in 1964. *Opposite:*
Doing a classic Black Ivy
mix: an unbuttoned, button-
down shirt and denim jacket,
in this instance a candy-
stripe shirt with a
Lee 91b jacket. **JJ**

Arthur Ashe

ARTHUR ROBERT ASHE, JR. (1943–1993)

Winning the US Open in 1968, Arthur Ashe was the number one tennis amateur in the country and viewed as the most promising player in the world. However, over 90 percent of the tennis and country clubs in the US had Whites Only policies. This meant that while he could compete and also train in them, Ashe could never become a club member. As such, he was challenging the status quo just by virtue of assuming he was entitled to play tennis, never mind winning. **JJ**

Not since the great Althea Gibson in the late '50s had a Black tennis player won any major tennis tournaments. And so, against a backdrop of civil unrest—heightened by the assassination of Martin Luther King that same year —the quiet, almost stoic player was both a hero and an anathema. Years later he revealed that his early mentor, Dr Robert R Johnson, Althea Gibson's former coach, had advised him to be 'unfailingly polite on the court and unfalteringly calm and detached so that whites could never accuse me of meanness.' As a result, he elected to allow his playing, his gentlemanly demeanour, and his consummate sense of style to talk for him. **JJ**

Ashe, photographed by John G. Zimmerman, goes unrecognized in the New York subway the day after he won the US open in 1968. He looks the business in a uniquely '60s sports inspired outfit in Ivy style. Notice the fine knit short sleeve V neck jersey he layers over his shirt. On his feet are a fine pair of beef-roll loafers, probably made by Sebago. **GM**

It's impossible to underestimate the importance of sportswear within contemporary Black culture, and while many would like us to believe that its origins date back to the birth of hip hop, wearing sportswear as casual wear precedes that period by some time. The Varsity jacket was an essential item on college campuses throughout the US in the '50s and '60s, showing allegiance to your team, fraternity or school. However, within Black culture at the time it demonstrated more than that. In a period where education was a political minefield with segregationists determined to prevent Black kids from entering all-white schools in the South, the Varsity jacket for African Americans was also a political assertion. This goes some way to explain why it's such a key part of the culture then and has had something of a resurgence in popularity within African-American culture at this moment in time, too. Here's college basketball legend **LEW ALCINDOR/KAREEM ABDUL-JABBAR (B.1947)** in the late '60s surrounded by a group of fans, along with the heavyweight champion of the world at the time, Muhammad Ali. Like the fans, off the court, Alcindor wore Black Ivy. **JJ**

'We had to be seen because we had to be heard.'

Tommie Smith

Their Black power protest during the awards ceremony at the Olympic games in 1968 resulted in the immediate suspension of both **TOMMIE SMITH (B.1944)**, *left*, and **JOHN CARLOS (B.1945)**, *right*. Just as when they wore black leather gloves and removed their shoes on the award podium, when they returned home—and with the attention of the world on them—their clothing was a powerful statement all its own. Smith combined a soft shoulder jacket with turtle neck sweater and love beads, while Carlos wore a sports anorak and plaid shirt—their look heralding the end of Black Ivy's golden age as we know it. The mindset behind the civil rights movement was peaceful protest, in the hope of gaining equal rights and an end to segregation. But Carlos' and Smith's actions came from a different perspective, aligning with the Black Panthers. Very much like the opening line of James Brown's song released a year later, 'I Don't Want Nobody to Give Me Nothing (Open Up the Door, I'll Get It Myself)', echoing the sentiment of self-reliance and independence from a system that had failed to meet the civil rights movement even halfway. The new look would quickly come to reflect that new mindset. **JJ**

IN ADVERTISING

SOMEWHERE...AT THE END OF THE RAINBOW

Big dream. Made team.
Red-letter days go better refreshed.
Coca-Cola, never too sweet,
gives that special zing . . . refreshes best.

things go
better
with
Coke

Drink
Coca-Cola

Stay merry – refresh with Coke. It gives you a real lift, a real taste, a real dash of extra energy

things go
better
with
Coke

Drink
Coca-Cola

Publications like *Ebony* served a Black audience in a way that no maintream publications could. But it took Black Chicago ad man, Tom Burrell, in the late '60s to convince brands to create dedicated ads for the African-American market. Until then they simply replicated the mainstream white ads, replacing them with Black models. **JJ**

The Triple Life of T. M. Alexander, Jr.

He's got two successful careers and one successful family.

In the daylight hours, he's a stockbroker.

After five, he's a real estate entrepreneur responsible for some of the most creative housing in Atlanta.

In a 14 hour work day, Coca-Cola is one of the few relaxing things he has time for.

Whether he's checking out a mining stock or working out the financing of 70 brick townhouses, T. M. can always use a Coke.

He's found that things, big and little, go better with Coke.

That's because Coca-Cola has that special taste.

Coke has the taste you never get tired of. Even on your day off.

Things go better with Coke.

To get him eating out of your hand...
add this fresh, clean taste!

Having a little snack? Whether you dote on *piles* of groceries, or a somewhat smaller assortment—don't take a bite without 7-Up! This is the sparkling drink that keeps your taste buds awake—so you don't miss a single good flavor. No wonder everything tastes tastier! Girls: Don't worry if he's *always* hungry. Just be glad it's always 7-Up time! Nothing, nothing, nothing does it like Seven-Up!

What's great about these ads are the clothes and the colourways. Demonstrating an aspirational feel, they point to a simplified version of that dream that civil rights is trying to attain. JJ

now it's Pepsi-for those who think young

Today's active people would rather play than watch. They lead the modern, full life—full time. This is the life for Pepsi—light, clean-tasting Pepsi. In stores, at fountains, think young. Say "Pepsi, please!"

Sundown in Marlboro Country.

The end of another long day. But just the beginning of another good smoke. Another Marlboro . . . just as fresh as that first one this morning. The rich breed of tobaccos in Marlboro's Richmond, Va., recipe keeps this flavor awake and alert. The exclusive Selectrate® Filter keeps it mild. There's a man's world of flavor in Marlboro Country. Settle back, you get a lot to like.

Opposite: Marlboro consistently advertised in *Ebony* magazine throughout the '60s, using real athletes to sell their classic product line. Here, Ernie Banks relaxes in a suit with a presidential style pocket square in his jacket and a pair of split toe derby shoes, echoing the Black Ivy style. *Left:* Another example of the one-size-fits-all approach applied by the finest ad agencies in the US at the time. The Marlboro Man, originally created by agency Leo Burnett in 1954, is still the brand's most iconic figure. A symbol of Wild West individualism (reframed as 'Marlboro Country') he made his way onto the pages of *Ebony* magazine, no problem. *Ebony* had also run several stories about real-life African-American cowboys and ranchers, including Miles Davis' father who imported premium hogs from Europe and was the second richest African American in the State of Illinois. Today, this particular Black cowboy might have met with a response similar to Lil Nas X' *Old Town Road* reactionary backlash, of course. JJ

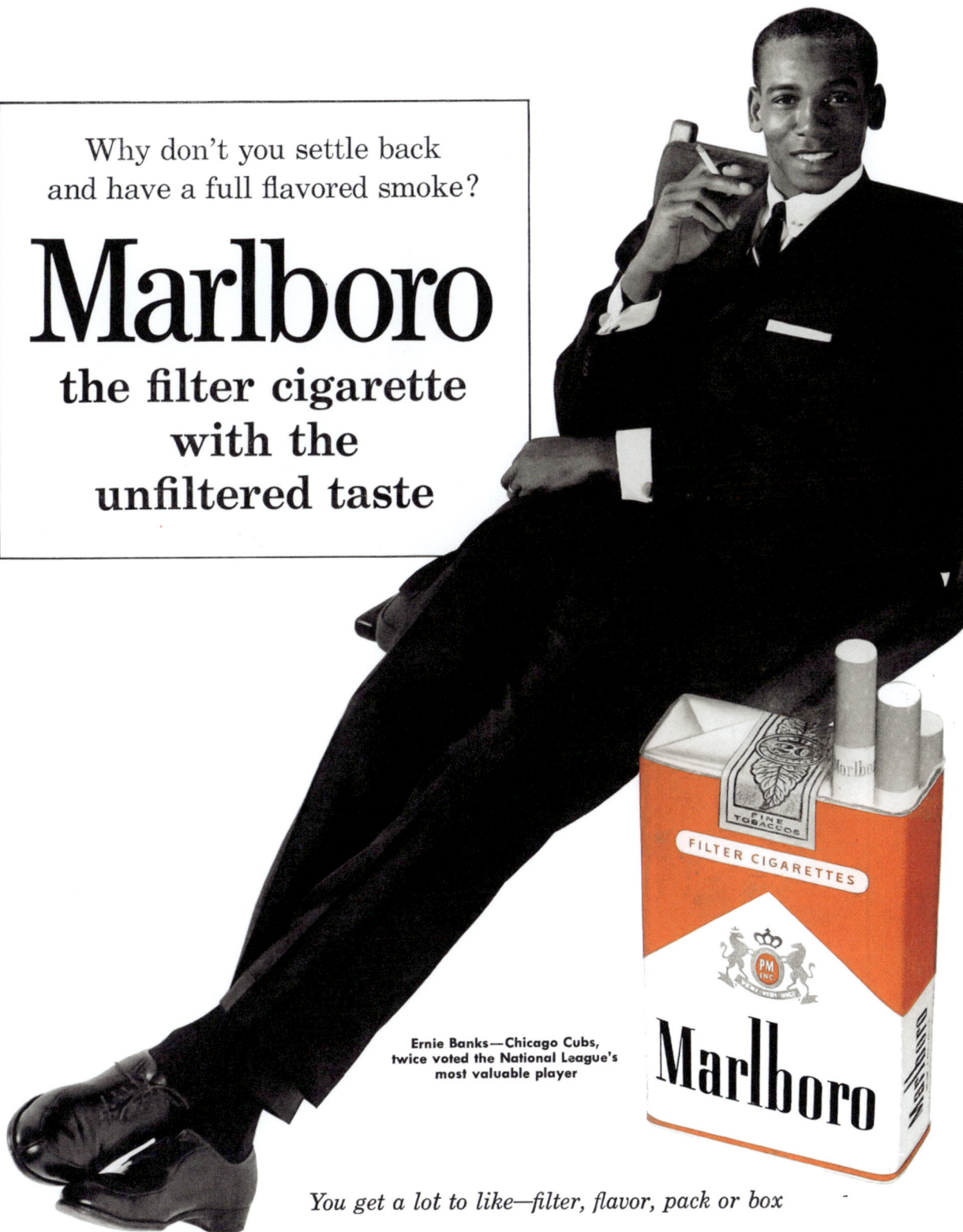

Why don't you settle back
and have a full flavored smoke?

Marlboro

the filter cigarette
with the
unfiltered taste

Ernie Banks—Chicago Cubs,
twice voted the National League's
most valuable player

FILTER CIGARETTES

FINE TOBACCOS

Marlboro

You get a lot to like—filter, flavor, pack or box

Tastes Great because the tobaccos are!

21 Great Tobaccos make 20 Wonderful Smokes!
CHESTERFIELD KING tastes great, smokes mild. You get 21 vintage tobaccos grown mild, aged mild and blended mild, and made to taste even milder through its longer length.

CHESTERFIELD KING

Tastes great, smokes mild... because the tobaccos are!

ORDINARY CIGARETTE

CHESTERFIELD KING

LONGER LENGTH means milder taste
The smoke of a Chesterfield King mellows and softens as it flows through longer length... becomes smooth and gentle to your taste.

real gusto in a great light beer
Schlitz

This one's more like it. Schlitz! Light, but all beer. Brewed, with just the kiss of the hops, to handle a big thirst lightly. How about one now? It's the beer that made Milwaukee famous simply because it tastes so good.

How in the world can a beer taste so big and drink so light? Because it's brewed with just the kiss of the hops. No more. No less. Get together with the beer that made Milwaukee famous simply because it tastes so good!

real gusto in a great light beer
Schlitz

"I'd walk a mile for a Camel."

This message is strictly for smokers who never tasted a Camel cigarette. Camel smokers, you know what we mean. You other guys, start walking.

CAMEL
TURKISH & DOMESTIC BLEND CIGARETTES

Left: Way more important than the cigarettes and alcohol advertised here is the particularly comfortable lifestyle these ads aim to reflect. Although essentially replicas of mainstream ads aimed at a Black audience, what they capture is a glimpse of a lifestyle where racism is no longer a factor. Should this be the only aspiration out there for African Americans? No, but perhaps it should be conceivable to experience without the barriers of prejudice if they so choose. *Opposite:* Attempting to capitalise on the civil rights movement's adoption of denim and dungerees, Lee made a concerted effort to court the African-American market. JJ

Any overall is made to take the tools . . . Only Lee is made to take the punishment!

Strain 'em. Scrape 'em. Grind 'em. Dig into the fabric with tools! Lee Bib Overalls stand up to wear and tear like no overalls made. Because they're the only overalls made of Lee's own exclusive Jelt® Denim . . . the hefty denim with 500 extra yards of yarn packed into it. 500 extra yards of yarn that dare you to make a hole. Dare you to rip a pocket. Dare you to bust a knee or a seat. And the strength of Lee's Sanforized Jelt Denim doesn't wash out. Where other overalls put starch, Lee puts extra yarn. And every pair gives you plenty of comfort features.

The shield back holds suspenders in place and eliminates body strain. The contoured front and back assure you free and easy movement. True, Lee costs a little more. But it's worth it. One thing, it proves you don't pinch pennies when it comes to quality. Or efficiency. And that says something about the kind of job you do yourself. Try a pair of Lee Bib Overalls. Next to you, they're the strongest thing in overalls. Lee work clothes...designed to fit you and your job.

Lee

H. D. Lee Company, Inc., Kansas City, Missouri
World's Largest Manufacturer of Union-Made Workwear

63

PHOTOGRAPHERS

ACKNOWLEDGEMENTS

JASON JULES First I'd like to thank Mariana—for your love, positivity, and patience. I'd also like to thank our two families—Ryan and Deanne, Doreen and Barry, and Anne Marie (my mum), as well as Jorge, Patricia, Ceci, Leti, and Guido.
Respect due to all those fighting for civil rights and equality around the world today

Special thanks to the Reel Art Press family—Tony, Ali, and Jack, for making it happen and keeping it fun.

And extra special thanks to Mr Graham Marsh, the coolest—and most knowledgeable—modernist I've ever met, and the man who believed this was a thing before anyone else.

Thanks to Kevin Rowland, Adam Rogers, Rebecca at Grey, Paul Tully, Constantine Weir, John Simons, Paul Simons, Jerry Dammers, Caryn Franklin, Ian Denyer, Jose Vincent, Caroline Conlon, Walé Adeyemi, Robert Elms, David Cohen, John Tinseth, Bolade Banjo, Lesley McKenley, Darren Statman, Paul Ayre, Fatsarazzi, Judah Afriyie, Tony Sylvester, Moteen, Michael Hill and everyone at Drakes, The Kchiporros family, Terry Ellis, Paul Weller, Remi Kabaka Jr, Tyrone Lebon, Christopher Bastin, Wayne Kirven, Jamie Ferguson, Raoul Shah, Michael Kopelman, Shawn Stussy, Moteen, Andrew Ibi, Julian Knox, Dawson Denim, Sandra Duncan, Leon Cerrone, Nick Clements, Takashi Okabe, Umar The Last Poets, Sergei Sviatchenko, Scott Fraser Simpson, Eddie Duffer, Horatio Shoes, Gordon The Urban Dandy, Acyde, Olu Michael Odukoya, Charlie Casely Hayford, Maria Casely Hayford, Kienda Hoji, Adrian Sykes, Shem, Mark Baxter, Monique Kawecki, Fred Nieddu, Steve Sane, Cyprian DeCoteau, Gerry Nelson, Willow Kaii, Will Milligan, Tim & Barry, Harris Elliott, Ranx, Xica Aires, Alan Richardson, Dave White Rag Top Vintage, Peter-Rene Lebenthal, Jamal Shabazz, Michael Bastian, Aleks Cvetkovic, Craig Ford, Greg Chapman, Simon Crompton, Lee McCormack , Rodney Nicholls, Simon Frederick, Chris Amfo, Paul Smith, Ralph Lauren, Brooks Brothers, Thom Browne, J Press, J Simons, Gant EU, Aaron Levine, Dr Ronx, Charlie Allen, Johnny Allen, Mick Dreher, Lena Dystant Terry Farley, Jo Wiser, Sonny Bussett, Dylan Jones, James Harvey Kelly, Harry The Pencil, Femi Fem, Gordon Ritchie, Justin Quirk, Nicholas Walter, Billy Prendergast, Harry Wilby, Ronald & Blaize, Hassan Hajjaj, Normski, Michelle Noel, Sarmilla (Ocha and Garth) and Lea Anderson. Special thanks to the Noah Purifoy Foundation.

CHECK OUT THE FOLLOWING ON INSTAGRAM, FOR MORE BLACK IVY STYLE AND SARTORIAL INSPIRATION:
Jay Gats **@jaygats**, Christopher Walker **@the_afro_preppy**, Shaun Gordon **@shaungordonstyle**, Elom **@elom_**,
Stephon Carson **@stephoncarson**, Avery Lucas **@mobydic.56**, Guy Tomlinson **@menofacertain**, André Larnyoh **@andretheapple**,
Black Menswear **@blackmenswear**, Bobby From Boston Vintage Store **@bobbyfromboston**, Harris Elliott **@harriselliottstudio**,
Sam & Shaka **@artcomesfirst**, Ignacio Quiles **@sartorialpairings**, Kiyanna Stewart and Jannah Handy **@blkmktvintage**,
Demetrius Harmon **@demetriusharmon**, Pythagore "Kraze Chelbe`" **@pythagore_hemingway_the_poet**,
Dandy Wellington **@dandywellington**, Acute Style **@acutestyle**, Kevis Manzi **@kevismanzi**, Armando Cabral **@armando_cabral**
Black Men With Style **@blackmenwithstyle**, Sem **@dapperclassic**, Walé **@acuratedman**, Karl-Edwin Guerre **@guerreisms**,
Jonathan **@milanstylelive**, Trevor Stuurman **@trevor_stuurman**, Renata Cherlise **@blackarchives.co**, C a r l · G **@carlsirtiger**,
Gabriel Akinosho **@gabrielakinosho**, Immanuel Sodipe **@kunle_x**, Torch Sportswear **@torchsportswear**,
Darren Johnston **@darrenj201**, Adolfo Loeri **@bourgiebudgetstyle**, Tremaine Emory **@denimtears**,
Samson Soboye **@soboye_boutique**, Ozwald Boateng **@ozwald_boateng**, Ouigi Theodore **@thebkcircus @thebkcircustokyo**

GRAHAM MARSH A tip of the beret to June Marsh, the Crew from the island, Max Katz, and Yoshio Sadasue.

SOME CLASSIC RETAILERS AND MAKERS:
American Classics **americanclassicslondon.com**, The Andover Shop **theandovershop.com**, Brooks Brothers **brooksbrothers.com**,
John Rushton Shoes **johnrushtonshoes.com**, John Simons **johnsimons.co.uk**, J. Press **jpressonline.com**, L.l.bean **llbean.com**,
Murray's Toggery Shop **nantucketreds.com**, O'connells **oconnellsclothing.com**, Ralph Lauren **ralphlauren.com**,
The Vintage Showroom **thevintageshowroom.com**, Alden **aldenshoe.com**, Bill's Khakis **billskhakis.com**, J. Keydge **jkeydge.com**,
Kamakura Shirts **kamakurashirts.com**, Mercer & Sons **mercerandsons.com**, Sanders Shoes **sanders-uk.com**

INDEX

PHOTO CREDITS

PUBLISHER TONY NOURMAND
TEXT JASON JULES
ART DIRECTOR GRAHAM MARSH
PHOTO RESEARCH & EDITOR JASON JULES & TONY NOURMAND
ADDITIONAL TEXT GRAHAM MARSH
DEPUTY ART DIRECTOR JACK CUNNINGHAM
MANAGING EDITOR ALISON ELANGASINGHE
PRE-PRESS HR DIGITAL SOLUTIONS
SPECIAL THANKS TO DAVE BROLAN

FIRST PUBLISHED 2021 BY REEL ART PRESS, AN IMPRINT OF RARE ART PRESS LTD., LONDON, UK

REELARTPRESS.COM

9 8 7 6 5 4 3 2 1

ISBN: 978-1-909526-82-2

PRINTED IN CHINA

FSC
www.fsc.org
MIX
Paper | Supporting
responsible forestry
FSC® C008047